# CONTENTS

# List of Illustrations

# GREAT AMERICAN
# HEROINES

# GREAT AMERICAN HEROINES

*BY ARNOLD DOLIN*

*ILLUSTRATED BY RAFAELLO BUSONI*

*Hart Publishing Company*

NEW YORK CITY

# POCAHONTAS
## *Brave Young Indian Princess*

THE FIRST SETTLERS who came to America were very brave people. They had to be brave, for danger faced them all the time. They never knew when the savage Indians would swoop down upon their little cabins and kill them all.

One of the bravest of these early settlers was Captain John Smith, the head of a small settlement in Virginia. One day when he was walking through the woods, he was captured by some Indians. They bound him and brought him to their chief.

The Indians gathered around as everything was made ready for his death. He was forced to kneel and place his head on the stump of a large tree.

As two terrible-looking savages stood over him

*. . . a cry was suddenly heard—and a lovely young
Indian maiden ran forward . . .*

with their tomahawks raised, a cry was suddenly heard —and a lovely young Indian maiden ran forward and threw her arms around Captain Smith's neck.

"Do not kill him," she begged. "He has done us no harm! Why do we not try to be his friend? I am sure he wants to be our friend."

The Indians put down their clubs, for they could not strike without killing the young girl, who was none other than the chief's daughter, Pocahontas. Again, she begged her father to save the white man's life.

Her plea was so touching and so earnest that her father gave in. He ordered Captain Smith's bonds to be removed and sent him back to his settlement.

This was the beginning of a long friendship between the Indians and the Virginia settlers. Pocahontas' courage will never be forgotten. And her simple gesture of friendship stands as a shining example in American history for peace and brotherhood among all men.

# ANNE HUTCHINSON
## *Defender of Religious Freedom*

MISTRESS HUTCHINSON drew her cloak about her and sat waiting tensely in the cold, bare New England church. She was on trial. She looked around the room at the faces of her friends and neighbors—the people she had known and loved so much during the three years since her arrival in the colony of Boston, Massachusetts, in 1634. But she could only find comfort in the honest, warm face of her husband, William. He alone still stood by her.

Why had the ministers of the church turned against her with such vengeance? She and her family, like all the other Puritans of the colony, had fled England for the cause of religious freedom. The King had refused to let these stern, God-fearing people practice their own religion as they wished, and instead, he had tried to force them to accept the Established Church of England. But now that these Puritans had found refuge in the New World, they were just as intolerant of other people who did not believe as they did.

Anne Hutchinson refused to accept this state of affairs. She did not like the way the Puritan Fathers were now persecuting others for their religious beliefs. She felt that church and state should be separate, rather than one strong body as it was here in Massachusetts, enforcing its religious and political will on all citizens. And she voiced her criticisms fearlessly.

Anne had organized a women's prayer meeting, where she discussed such problems. Often, she would comment on this or that sermon, noting the things with which she disagreed. Gradually, the colony came to be divided. The Puritan Fathers saw that they must deal with this woman, or risk the loss of their absolute authority.

So she was now on trial. For three weeks, she had argued with the ministers who served as her judges. She had quoted Scripture, text for text, with her accusers, attempting to show them that she was not just a stubborn, rebellious woman, but as great a lover of the Lord as they. But in her heart, she knew that they remained steadfast in their opposition.

Finally, Governor Winthrop faced her and asked, "Mistress Hutchinson, you have been accused of harboring evil opinions, of exercising a lying tongue, and of trafficking with the Devil. Will you forsake this wickedness and accept the authority of the church in all matters?"

Anne Hutchinson answered, "What you have said is not so. I have meant no evil. The Lord judgeth not as man judgeth. The Lord will not cast off His servant."

"Then the sentence of the court is that you are banished from Massachusetts as being a woman not fit for our society," proclaimed Governor Winthrop.

As if this cruel blow were not enough, Anne's beloved pastor, John Cotton, then arose and addressed her "In the name of our Lord Jesus Christ and in the name of the church, I do not only pronounce you worthy to be cast out, but I do cast you out; and in the name of Christ, I do deliver you up to Satan."

Her pastor had become her accuser. The people she had nursed in illness and comforted in sorrow would not or dared not defend her now. It was hard to accept such things. But Anne Hutchinson would not take the easy way out—she would not renounce what she believed was right just to resume her life in the colony.

When Anne and William returned home that evening, their sad faces broke the news to their children. The little ones wept. And young Francis, a devoted champion of his mother, said staunchly, "Do not grieve, Mother. We believe in you."

Anne was comforted. After the children had gone to sleep, she and her husband sat for a while by the fire, talking over plans for the future. "William, I am sorely troubled," Anne said. "Where shall we go now? Where can we lead a decent life and worship as we please? I humbly beg your forgiveness for the terrible hardship and shame I have brought upon you and the children."

"There is nothing to forgive," her good husband answered. "We are all proud of you. As for our future home, I have heard many wonderful things about the new colony in Rhode Island. When young Roger Williams was cast out of Massachusetts for preaching religious freedom, he founded a settlement which he called Providence, in thankfulness to the Lord for protecting him. He welcomes everyone to the colony, no matter what church he belongs to. I believe we could live there peaceably and happily."

So William built a house at Portsmouth. During their first year there, a grievous illness fell upon Anne. Yet, even in sickness, she evoked no sympathy from the Puritans of Massachusetts. Instead, she received word that when the people of Boston learned of her misfortune, they said, "Verily, this punishment proves that she is a child of Satan."

She rallied all her energies to disprove the slander. And by the tender care of her family, she was nursed back to strength. Anne believed it was the Lord who had restored her health, and she rejoiced in her faith.

The next few years were happy and fruitful. William had become Judge Hutchinson, an important and respected member of the new colony.

Then a delegation arrived from the Boston church. They came to call on William and his wife, who greeted them courteously but coldly. One of the ministers spoke: "Mistress Hutchinson, we bring a message from the Lord and His church."

Her reply was brief and to the point: "There be many lords. I acknowledge but one. What lord do *you* mean?"

One of the ministers haughtily continued, "We come in the name of the one God. Now that you have had time to think over your sins, we ask you to renounce your evil teachings and abide by the word of the church."

Anne Hutchinson remained steadfast. "That will I not do," she said simply.

The ministers returned to Boston. Their wrath grew and the news from Massachusetts was ominous. Anne heard that the Boston government was attempting to extend its authority to Rhode Island. When her devoted husband died, she decided to leave her home rather than face another enforced exile, should the Puritans succeed in gaining control of Rhode Island.

With her son Francis and her six other children, Anne migrated to a small Dutch settlement on the wooded shores of Pelham Bay, near what is now New York City—far, far away from the religious quarrels of Puritan New England. Anne was satisfied that at last there they would be free from religious persecution.

But the valiant family now faced a new kind of danger. Their home, deep in the wilderness, a lonely log cabin surrounded by forests, was a mile from the nearest neighbor. And the colony was involved in fierce Indian wars.

There had never been any great trouble with the Indians in Boston. Anne had always thought of the Indians as strange, silent creatures whose bodies she could nourish with a crust of bread and whose poor heathen souls she could save with the message of God. Her warm, generous heart never allowed her to fear these people, but instead, prompted her to help them in every way.

One day, she heard on Indian warwhoop ringing through the woods. To her it was a new sound and she hardly knew what it meant. At any rate, there was no one she could call to for help.

Suddenly, the woods seemed to be full of yelling savages. Anne quickly gathered her children about her, ran into the cabin and bolted the door. As she peered through the windows, she could see a band of redskins, faces smeared with war paint, menacingly swinging their tomahawks. The Hutchinsons stood huddled together frightened stiff; in a few minutes, the Indians had smashed down the door, rushed into the cabin, and carried off Anne and her children.

Only the youngest daughter, Susan, lived to tell the tale of that terrible day. The rest were all massacred.

Today, the people of Boston, as well as the millions

*. . . Governor Winthrop faced her, ". . . you have
been accused of . . . trafficking with the Devil."*

*. . . she could see a band of redskins . . . swinging*
*their tomahawks.*

throughout the rest of our great land, find it difficult to understand the bitterness of these old religious quarrels. It is difficult to conceive that they who had fled from religious persecution should themselves have turned persecutors. Free believers in freedom revere the name of Anne Hutchinson as one who laid the foundation for one of our most precious freedoms—freedom of belief.

# "MAD ANN" BAILEY
## Fearless Frontier Woman

THE INDIANS were on the warpath. Fort Lee was surrounded. Only a garrison outpost in what was frontier wilderness in 1791, Fort Lee had little hope of rescue. The nearest white men were many miles away. Hundreds of redskins, decked out in warpaint and feathers, rode around the stockade, whooping blood-curdling war cries and brandishing tomahawks. Barrages of arrows hissed through the air. Many of them pierced the walls of the stockade.

The band of white settlers inside the garrison were safe as long as they could hold off the Indians with their firepower. But if they slackened their rifle fire for any length of time, they were sure to be overrun by the savages. Then it would be the same old story, one that had already become a familiar part of frontier history—brutal, horrible massacre of every white man, woman, and child.

The white men fought bravely and hoped against hope. But soon they had to face the terrible truth: their supply of gunpowder was beginning to run dangerously low. The Captain of the garrison called together the people and told them frankly just what a predicament they were all in.

"Folks, I'd like to be able to say, 'Don't worry, we can fight off these heathens.' But I might as well be honest and square with you. In another day—maybe two—we won't have any gunpowder left. If we try to use it sparingly now, the Indians might get some notions and storm our barricades. We can't possibly hold them off indefinitely. And when they're as riled as they seem to be now, they don't give up without a knock-down, drag-out fight."

One woman, with a terrified look on her face, screamed, "But my children . . . my babies . . . what will they do to them?"

The Captain urged the people not to panic, and then turned to the woman to try to reassure her, but there was little he could say. "Ma'am, we'll do everything within our power to protect all of you. After that, we might as well just pray to the good Lord and hope he sees fit to send us some help."

Suddenly, another woman's voice was heard, a brave,

strong voice: "We ain't been licked yet! I'll ride out and bring back more ammunition."

A chorus of protest arose: "No! No!"

And a grizzled old veteran of many Indian battles shouted, "It's sure death—and worse than that. If the Indians get you, they won't just kill you outright. They'll scalp you or torture you, and do all sorts of savage things."

The Captain spoke again. "The lady who volunteered—what's your name?"

"Ann Bailey," she answered proudly.

A respectful silence followed. They all knew the name. She was "Mad Ann" Bailey, the almost legendary heroine of the frontier—the woman who was called "mad" because of her complete lack of fear, the woman who lived only to get revenge against the "redskin varmints" who had killed her first husband.

All eyes turned on her. Those who had only heard of the fantastic tales of her feats of daring and skill were surprised at what they saw. Almost fifty years old at that time, Ann Bailey was short and stout. She wore rough clothes—men's clothes—and at the belt of her buckskin breeches she carried a butcher's knife and a tomahawk. It was hard to believe that this short, stumpy creature could be the woman who was famous throughout West Virginia as a crack shot, a superb horsewoman, and a woodsman whose knowledge and craft were hardly equaled by white man or redskin.

Ann Bailey had been born in Liverpool, England, the daughter of a soldier who had fought under the famous Duke of Marlborough. When her parents died, she managed to get passage to America, and went to live with relatives in Virginia's Shenandoah Valley. There she married a frontiersman, Richard Trotter, who was later killed in a fierce battle with the Indians at Point Pleasant. From that day on, she seemed to have no other ambition than to avenge her husband's death. Married now to John Bailey, a leading frontiersman of West Virginia, she pooh-poohed the idea that a woman's place was in the home and continued her adventures, treating her numerous narrow escapes from death as though they were all just part of a game. Her phenomenal luck led the Indians to believe that she was mysteriously protected by the Great Spirit, and because of this superstition, some even refused to shoot at her. Many white settlers too became convinced that she led a charmed life.

So why not let "Mad Ann" Bailey attempt to ride out of the garrison and search for help? If anyone could rescue them from this desperate situation, it must be this fearless woman.

"Mrs. Bailey," said the Captain, "we all seem to be in agreement. You are our one hope. May God protect you on this mission."

And so she rode off. The settlers watched and waited. How could Ann ever manage to slip through without attracting the attention of all those Indians? It was a foolhardy idea, but . . . . The men in the garrison did all they could by laying down a heavy barrage of rifle fire. Somehow, miraculously, Ann Bailey got through the Indian lines!

But this was only the beginning of a journey that would have taxed the strength, courage, and cunning of the hardiest of men. There was no road to follow— Ann had to make her way through forests, up mountains, across streams. No one will ever really know how she managed to find her way.

But find her way she did—over more than one hundred miles of what would have been impassable terrain for most anyone else. Finally, she reached Fort Savannah in Pennsylvania. She told her story quickly, impressing the garrison commander with the urgency of the need at Fort Lee. They brought her another horse to be led behind her own; they packed as much gunpowder on this horse as he could possibly carry. And then she was off again, leaving behind an admiring band of soldiers.

Meanwhile, the settlers had just about given up hope. They had used up almost all the gunpowder. Food and water were running low. Most of the men had not slept for days. The attacks were becoming more and more ferocious. It seemed unlikely that Ann Bailey would return in time, if at all.

One day; a soldier at the lookout post gave the word.

The news circulated wildly throughout the stockade: a lone woman and two horses had been sighted several miles away. It *had* to be Ann! Could she get back through the line of besieging Indians? The next hour was filled with almost unbearable suspense.

A little while later, "Mad Ann" rode through the door of the stockade. A mighty cheer arose. Relief, jubilation, and gratitude—they were all heard in that great roar of welcome.

The gunpowder was distributed. The Captain drew up a plan of action. They were to maintain their light rifle fire throughout the night, so that the Indians would not suspect they had received reinforcements. The next morning there was to be a massive surprise attack.

The strategy worked, and the Indians were completely routed. The few who were not killed gave up and disappeared into the forest. Fort Lee and its inhabitants had been saved.

As a small token of their gratitude, the people gave Ann the swiftest and handsomest horse they could buy. She named him Liverpool, for the city of her birth, and the two of them remained inseparable until the black steed could no longer run. When the Indians heard about Ann's great exploit, they named her *The White Squaw of Kanawha,* for Fort Lee was located on the Kanawha River.

After the Indian troubles died down, Ann Bailey

. . . "Mad Ann" rode through the door of the
stockade. A mighty cheer arose.

began a mail and package service among the settlements. A wonderful storyteller of true adventure tales, she was a welcome guest wherever she went.

When her second husband died, Ann was sixty years old. She never lost her tremendous vitality; and even when she reached eighty, she thought nothing of walking twenty miles to visit friends. "Mad Ann" Bailey will be remembered as the most fearless woman of American colonial times.

# BETSY ROSS
## *Mother of Our Flag*

"MOTHER, MOTHER!" Clarissa called, "General Washington's carriage has just stopped in front of our shop. I think he's coming to call on you!"

Betsy Ross was upstairs, working on new upholstery that she was sewing for the sofa in her sitting room. Her hair needed fixing, and her hands were full of pins and scissors and measuring tape. It was no way in which to receive the Commander-in-Chief of the Colonial Army. And if the busy General was taking time out to visit her shop, then it must indeed be on an important matter. Though how he could be concerned with her—a young widow who made her living as a seamstress—Betsy could scarcely imagine.

Hurriedly, she tidied herself up as best she could,

and then went downstairs. She saw that General Washington was accompanied by two other men, Colonel George Ross, her husband's uncle, and Robert Morris, the wealthy Philadelphia banker who was helping to finance the Revolutionary War. Though nervous and flustered, she received them graciously and respectfully. But she couldn't stop wondering why these distinguished gentlemen had called on *her*.

General Washington quickly came to the point. "Mrs. Ross, can you make a flag for us?"

Somewhat taken aback, Betsy Ross hardly knew how to answer. But she heard herself saying, "Why . . . I've never made one before . . . but I can try, Sir. It will be a very great honor for me to sew a flag for our country."

"Good. I admire your spirit, Madame," Washington replied, "the kind of spirit we need to win this war, and gain our independence. When we talked about a flag yesterday, Colonel Ross said you would be just the person for the job. I can see that he was right."

"Thank you, General. I hope I prove worthy of your confidence," Betsy said.

"I'm sure you shall," answered Washington. "You know the importance of a flag. Many people might scoff at our making so much of just a scrap of cloth. But throughout recorded history, men have fought and died for a scrap of cloth when it symbolized the cause they were fighting for. We need such a symbol around which our men can rally."

Betsy Ross was moved by this great man's words. An ardent American patriot, she was happy for the chance of making a contribution to the cause she believed in so deeply. Her father had helped to build Independence Hall in Philadelphia. Her husband, a member of the Pennsylvania Militia, had been killed in the war just five months ago.

"Do you have a design for the flag?" she asked.

Colonel Ross spoke. "Yes, Betsy, we do. We colonists have been inventing all sorts of flags just to have some kind of banner under which to fight against the Redcoats. Ships have displayed flags with the New York emblem of the beaver. General Washington's ship has flown a pine-tree flag. Others have carried a device showing a bunch of thirten arrows held in a fish. One of the most popular flags has borne a rattlesnake with thirteen rattles and the motto "Don't Tread on Me." But none of these standards has truly caught the spirit embodied in our Declaration of Independence. We have tried in our new design to produce a flag which embodies the spirit and unity of all thirteen colonies proudly fighting together."

Then Washington drew a sheet of paper from his pocket, unrolled it, and displayed the sketch to Mrs. Ross. It consisted of a rectangular field of blue in the upper left-hand corner on which there were thirteen white stars. The rest of the banner showed thirteen stripes of alternating red and white.

"The white stars indicate the unity of the thirteen colonies," he said.

"Blue is a strong color, and white stands for purity," added Robert Morris.

"And red is the color of courage," said Colonel Ross.

Betsy Ross felt as though they were reciting a sacred ritual. She liked the design very much, but thought there was some room for improvement. When asked by General Washington whether she had any suggestions, she surprised herself with her own boldness: "I think, Sir, that it would be more pleasing to the eye if the stars were arranged in a circle rather than being scattered. It would also make a clearer symbol of unity."

And General Washington replied, "I believe you are right. Anything else, Mrs. Ross?"

"Well . . . yes. Don't you think that a five-pointed star would look better than this six-pointed one?" she asked.

All three gentlemen agreed with her, but then Robert Morris asked, "Won't it be more difficult for you to make a five-pointed star?"

Whereupon Betsy Ross folded a piece of paper and, with a few snips of her scissors, produced a perfect five-pointed star.

General Washington spoke again. "Then we are now in complete agreement. We are indebted to you, Madame, for your excellent suggestions. We shall depend

*Then Washington . . . displayed the sketch to
Mrs. Ross.*

on you."

Betsy Ross went to work, carefully measuring and cutting and sewing. The finest gown of the most beautiful silks had never commanded such loving care as did this simple red, white, and blue cotton flag.

When the flag was completed, it was run up the mast of a vessel on the Delaware River. Later, the flag was carried into the Hall of Congress for inspection, and there it was approved as the official American flag.

After the summer of 1777, *The Star-Spangled Banner* was held aloft wherever American troops went, on land or on sea. The famous naval hero, John Paul Jones, hoisted the newborn banner when he was appointed commander of his ship *The Ranger.* He later wrote: "The flag and I were born on the same day and hour. We are twins and cannot be separated in life or death. So long as we can float, we shall float together. If we must sink, we shall go down together."

Betsy Ross was rewarded with a contract to make all the flags for the new government, and this contract continued long after the Revolutionary War was won. When she died at the age of 84, her daughter, Clarissa, carried on her art of flagmaking.

There are now fifty stars in the flag of the United States representing the fifty states of the Union. But the basic design remains the same as that sewed by Betsy Ross.

# MOLLY PITCHER
## Cannoneer of the Revolution

"OH, HOW I'd like to be a soldier!" You often hear
young men or boys say that, but seldom young girls.
But Mary Ludwig, whom everyone called Molly, really
felt that way.

The American Revolutionary War had just started.
Everywhere, young men were joining the army.

"Why do men get a chance to fight for their country, and not women? I have to stay here and cook and
clean, while the men go off and fight!"

Her friends laughed at her impatience, but they
liked her for it. There was one young man, though, who
fell in love with her. His name was John Hays, and he
was a handsome fellow. A few months after they were
married, he came home one evening to tell her he had

joined the Continental Army.

"If I can't go myself, I'm proud to be a soldier's wife! May God bless you!" said Molly. So she kissed her husband good-by, he went off to the war, and she went back to her housework.

Months went by, and she did not hear from him. Then one day as she was working in the field, a man on horseback came galloping toward her. He had a letter from her husband, who was now a cannoneer with the American forces. In the letter, John Hays asked Molly to go to her father's farm. The army was camped near there, and her husband could more easily get to see her if she were there.

Molly was overjoyed. She packed her few belongings and set out. Her husband, John, sometimes visited her at her father's farm; but of course, she did not get to see him often.

One day, she heard the sound of guns and cannons. "A battle must be going on!" she thought. "I must get there!"

It was a very hot day in June. The temperature was almost 100 degrees. When Molly arrived at the battlefield, she saw that many soldiers were overcome by heat and thirst. Quickly, she took a bucket and ran to a nearby stream to fill it. No sooner had she given water to one poor soldier, than another one would call out, "Molly, the pitcher! Please!"

All day long, in the thick of battle, Molly carried

*. . . picking up the rammer, she loaded the cannon and fired.*

water to the hot and thirsty and to the wounded. All day long they would call, "Molly, bring the pitcher!" Many of the soldiers did not know who she was. It is easy to see how she won her nickname, *Molly Pitcher.*

Suddenly, Molly saw her husband fall forward over his cannon. She ran to his side and laid her hand on his heart. It was still beating. She called two soldiers and had them carry him under a shady tree. She bathed his forehead with cold water, for she could see that he had been overcome by the heat. Just then she heard General Greene, the American commander, say, "Remove the cannon. We have no gunner to take Hays's place!"

"No!" cried Molly. "Let me fire the cannon. I will serve in my husband's place!" And picking up the rammer, she loaded the cannon and fired.

All day long she stayed at her post, and when finally the enemy had been driven back, General Greene strode over to where Molly stood. "I thank you in the name of the American Army!" he said. And all the soldiers cheered, "Hurray for Captain Molly!"

So it was that Molly became a soldier. Her country will never forget her courage.

# BARBARA FRIETCHIE
## *Defender of "Old Glory"*

"I SAY THEY'LL come plumb through the town, plunderin' and murderin'. And I say we best get out, now, while the gettin' is good." The white-haired man pounded his fist into the palm of his hand as he spoke, and the others listened.

"Where'll we go?" a younger man asked.

"We'll go north, north. Where do you think we'll go?"

The younger man shook his head. "There'll be no room for us up north of here, Jonathan. You know that. What shelter there is will go for the Union wounded. We just got to stay here, as I see it."

The small group of men who were standing on the street corner all agreed with the younger man, but old

Jonathan wouldn't be quiet.

"This Stonewall Jackson is a devil in human flesh," Jonathan said, and his hands trembled now as he spoke. "If you want your womenfolk abused and your homes burned, and if you want to be shot yourselves, you stay. But mark my words, the town of Frederick won't be here tomorrow nor anyone that's in it. I'm goin'." With that, the old man hurried off.

Suddenly, all the men in the group turned around. Down the main street of the town ran fifteen-year-old Billy Farnsworth. He was shouting.

"They'll be here before noon! They'll be here before noon!" he called.

As the boy came alongside of the group, one of the men stopped him. "How do you know, lad?"

"The mail just came in, and the rider said he saw them only a few miles off." The boy was so excited he could hardly speak. "There's thousands of them. And Stonewall Jackson's out in front!"

The men would have liked to ask him more, but Billy Farnsworth hurried off, shouting the news. As the townspeople heard him, the doors of shops and houses opened. Little bunches of men and women began to collect on the street.

Soon, everyone seemed to be talking at once, breaking off now and then to look toward the south. But nothing could be seen. The little town of Frederick, Maryland, was surrounded by green, rolling, beautiful hills that blocked the view.

Finally, someone shouted, "There's the Mayor! Let's hear what he has to say."

Mayor Roberts was standing on the porch of his house, and all the small groups of people crowded around him. The Mayor raised his hands for silence. His voice was serious but steady.

"You all probably know by now," Mayor Roberts said, "that Stonewall Jackson and his rebel army are marching on Frederick. I hear some of you say we should leave the town and go north. To that, I'd say fine—for those of you who are rich or have friends to go to. But for those of us who are common people, I say, *stay here!* I know as well as you that Stonewall Jackson is a hard man, but I say that if we act properly toward him and his soldiers, he'll spare us."

The Mayor stopped to see how his ideas were being received. Everyone was listening carefully. So he went on.

"First of all, my friends, we've got to show him we mean him no harm. How'll we do that? For one thing, stay off the streets. And also, take down *The Stars and Stripes.* I know that may sound cowardly, but we're not soldiers here. We don't mean to fight, and there's no sense in irritating these rebels. Especially this Stonewall Jackson. Well, what do you say, my friends?"

For a moment, there was no answer. Suddenly, someone shouted; "Yes, take down *The Stars and Stripes!*

Then everyone else joined in.

The crowd began to chatter, and everyone was more cheerful now. Groups of men went off to take the flags from the post office and the schoolhouse. What few flags were flying from private houses quickly disappeared.

As noon approached, the townspeople went into their homes.

Then the dull rumble of hundreds of horses' hoofs and thousands of men's marching feet rose in the distance. General Stonewall Jackson was at the southern end of town with his army. The year was 1862, and the Civil War—the terrible war that Americans were fighting between themselves over the question of slavery and secession—was rolling over Maryland.

Some of the townspeople had hidden themselves in cellars. Some were shaking with fear in closets. Some braver ones were crouching timidly behind their curtains, peering out of their windows for a look at the soldiers.

There they were, thousands of them in their gray uniforms, some marching, some riding, carrying rifles and packs, pistols and sabers, drawing cannons and supplies. At their head rode a fierce-looking, bearded man. His face was stern and hard, his eyes bright, and his glance steady. He rode a fine, strong stallion with the ease and grace of an expert horseman. He was a soldier from the tips of his polished boots to the peak of his Confederate campaign hat. Everyone who saw him knew immediately that this must be Stonewall Jackson.

The army had reached the middle of town, and still no signal had been given for violence. The Mayor, who stood behind his closed door, congratulated himself on having lowered the flags. It looked as though the rebels would pass through the town and do no damage at all.

Then, suddenly, a terrible and wonderful thing happened—something no one expected. John Greenleaf Whittier wrote a famous poem describing it:

> *Up rose old Barbara Frietchie then,*
> *Bowed with her fourscore years and ten;*
> *Bravest of all in Frederick town,*
> *She took up the flag the men hauled down;*
> *In her attic window the flag was set,*
> *To show that one heart was loyal yet.*

The townspeople across the street who watched and saw what had happened were thunderstruck. They couldn't believe their eyes. There, from Barbara Frietchie's attic window, hung *The Stars and Stripes!* Who could have put it there? Certainly not aged Barbara Frietchie herself, that feeble, wrinkle-faced woman, ninety years old!

> *Up the street came the rebel tread,*
> *Stonewall Jackson riding ahead.*
> *Under his slouched hat left and right*

*He glanced: the old flag met his sight.*
*"Halt!"—the dust brown ranks stood fast;*
*"Fire!"—out blazed the rifle blast.*
*It shivered the window, pane and sash;*
*It rent the banner with seam and gash.*

The Union flag folded and was about to fall to the ground.

*Quick, as it fell, from the broken staff*
*Dame Barbara snatched the silken scarf;*
*She leaned far out on the window-sill,*
*And shook it forth with a royal will.*

There was no doubt left in anyone's mind now who had put the flag there. Barbara's voice, cracked with age, would not have been heard except that the rebel ranks stood motionless in amazement.

*"Shoot, if you must, this old gray head,*
*But spare your country's flag," she said.*

Stonewall Jackson stared up at the ancient woman. His eyes burned. Color rose from his neck and reddened his cheeks. He was a soldier—and one of the finest that the South possessed. He knew the meaning of bravery. When he had first reached the town of Frederick, although he had said nothing to his lieutenants, he had felt contempt for these Northerners who had hidden their flags. But here was the fighting spirit! Here was the spirit he had met in the Union troops on the battlefield. Without turning his head, he gave the order:

*"Who touches a hair of yon gray head*
*Dies like a dog! March on!" he said.*

*"She leaned far out on the window-sill . . ."*

The Southern troops began to move again, raising the dust of the street as they went. Barbara Frietchie held the flag from her window until the last rebel soldier had passed underneath and out of Frederick. When finally the danger was gone, the townspeople came from their hiding places. Those who hadn't seen were told what Barbara Frietchie had done.

Word of her valor spread through the South as well as the North, and all who heard gave honor to a brave American.

# DOLLY MADISON
## *Most Popular First Lady*

AS HER CARRIAGE approached the imposing structure of Morris House in Philadelphia, the home of President and Mrs. George Washington, the young lady's excitement mounted. As a member of Philadelphia society, she had, of course, met the Washingtons on several occasions. But never before had she been summoned for a private meeting with the gracious First Lady, and she wondered why such attention was being accorded to her.

Not yet twenty-six, Dolly Payne Todd was a beautiful widow—tall and statuesque, with blue eyes, dark curls, and rosy cheeks. Her husband had died only a year earlier during the yellow-fever epidemic. Though she had loved John Todd dearly, Dolly was much too young, attractive, and full of the joy of living to remain a widow. Already, she was the object of keen competition among most of the eligible bachelors of the city.

When the butler showed Dolly into the elegant drawing room, Martha Washington came forward to greet her. "My dear Dolly, how good of you to come. Ah, you look lovely as ever! It's so good for these old eyes of mine to feast on such youthfulness and charm."

And the two women began to chat about this and that social event, inquiring after the health of friends and relatives. Martha Washington poured tea for her guest, and then she suddenly asked, "Tell me, Dolly, is it true that you are engaged to marry James Madison?"

The color rose in Dolly's cheeks making her even more radiant than before. She was confused and a bit embarrassed. *Had the modest, shy Mr. Madison asked the First Lady to use her persuasive powers for his proposal?* She hesitated and then said, "Truthfully, I have not yet made up my mind. I've known Mr. Madison only a short time; and as you remember, it is not yet a year since my beloved husband was buried. I am greatly honored by Mr. Madison's proposal, and yet I cannot be sure that this would be a proper marriage for either of us."

"Forgive me for meddling, my girl," Martha Washington replied, "but I do want to tell you how highly

*"Tell me, Dolly, is it true that you
are engaged . . .?"*

General Washington and I esteem James Madison, and how very happy it would make us to see him married to you. I'm sure you must have your pick of many more romantic men, but there is none who will love and cherish you more. He has a great future in our government, and he needs a wife like you."

Dolly was very much touched by the First Lady's sentiments, and she went home to give the matter serious consideration. Certainly, she had nothing but respect and admiration for James Madison, who was hailed throughout the colonies as the *Father of the Constitution*. And she was not concerned by the fact that he was not particularly handsome. After further meetings, she came to know James Madison as a truly gentle and warm person with a fine sense of humor, and soon she developed a genuine affection for him.

And so they were married on September 15, 1794. Now the wife of the "great little Madison" (as he was called by the people) and sponsored by no less a personage than President Washington's First Lady, Dolly occupied a high place in Philadelphia society. Her husband was the friend and protégée of Thomas Jefferson, Washington's first Secretary of State. Moreover, Jefferson was an old friend and beau of Dolly's mother, and he was almost like an uncle to Dolly. For three years, the Madisons attended exciting lunches, receptions, dinners, and balls. Dolly was in the center of political activity, and she became friendly with the most powerful people in the government.

During John Adams' term of office as President, Dolly and James Madison lived quietly on the family plantation in Virginia. But when Thomas Jefferson was elected President, he appointed Madison to serve as his Secretary of State. The capital city had now been moved to Washington, along the banks of the Potomac River. Since both Jefferson and Vice President Aaron Burr were widowers, it was logical that Dolly Madison should assume the role of official hostess in the President's House. It was a role she was perfectly equipped for, and she filled it magnificently. She was always dressed tastefully and in the height of fashion. She entertained rival senators, Cabinet members, and foreign diplomats—charming them all with her warmth, friendliness, and perfect tact. She was beautiful, gay, witty, clever, charming. No one could resist this dazzling lady.

When Jefferson had served for two terms and declined to run again, his natural successor seemed to be James Madison. Dolly's efforts had strengthened her husband's political alliances, and with Jefferson's backing, Madison was elected the fourth President of the United States.

Now truly the *First Lady of the Land,* Dolly outdid herself. She redecorated the interior of the President's House, and then gave a brilliant reception. A thousand candles glowed throughout the house; the Marine

Band, in scarlet uniforms, played music for the guests. And dessert after dinner was a delightful surprise— *ice cream,* a delicacy new to the American colonies.

But during Madison's second term, more serious events occurred. America was again at war with England. During the summer of 1814, a large British landing party put ashore at Chesapeake Bay. They routed the American forces and advanced on Washington. President Madison hastened to join the American troops outside the city. When the news reached Dolly that the British were marching on Washington and were due to arrive at any time, she was practically alone in the house, with only a few servants. While waiting for her husband to return, she sat down and calmly wrote the following letter to her sister, describing the events of those terrible days:

*Tuesday, August 23, 1814*

My dear Sister:

My husband left me yesterday to join General Winder . . . I have since received two dispatches from him . . . he desires that I should be ready at a moment's warning to enter my carriage and leave the city . . . I am accordingly ready; I have pressed as many Cabinet Papers into trunks as will fill one carriage; our private property must be sacrificed, as it is impossible to procure wagons for its transporta-

tion. I am determined not to go myself until I see
Mr. Madison safe.

My friends and acquaintances are all gone—even
Colonel C., with his hundred men, who were sta-
tioned as guards.

*Wednesday, 3 o'clock* . . . We have had a battle
near Bladensburg, Maryland, and I am still here,
within sound of the cannon! Mr. Madison comes
not; may God protect him! Two messengers, cov-
ered with dust, bid me fly; but I wait for him . . . At
this late hour a wagon has been procured; I have
had it filled with the plate and most valuable porta-
ble articles belonging to the house.

Our kind friend, Mr. Carroll, has come to hasten
my departure, and is in a very bad humor with me
because I insist on waiting until the large picture of
General Washington is secured, and it requires to be
unscrewed from the wall. This process was found to
be too tedious for these perilous moments; I have
therefore ordered the frame to be broken, and the
canvas taken out; it is done—and the precious portrait placed in the hands of two gentlemen from
New York for safe keeping.

And now, dear sister, I must leave this house . . .
When I shall see or write you, or where I shall be
tomorrow, I cannot tell.

Dressed as a farmer's wife and servant, Dolly and

her maid were bundled into the wagon and driven off by a soldier. Gunpowder smoke filled the air, and there were loud shouts of "Washington is lost to the enemy!" But Dolly took heart from the fact that one particular Washington was not lost—the famous oil painting of George Washington made by Gilbert Stuart, one of America's greatest artists. She also carried with her the original copy of the Declaration of Independence.

The roads were clogged with people fleeing the burning city, but no one noticed the humble figure in the little wagon. If they had, they would scarcely have dreamed that she was the glamorous Dolly Madison or that she carried with her some of the nation's most priceless treasures. She spent that night in a tent, gazing across the Potomac at the flames rising from the city of Washington—flames that were destroying such buildings as the Capitol, the Library of Congress, and the President's House.

Dolly rejoined her husband the next day, and three days later they returned to Washington, after the enemy had left the ravaged city. Many people considered it useless to attempt to rebuild the city, and urged Madison to move the government back to Philadelphia. Dolly was furious at this suggestion. "Shall we let the British drive us out of our own capital city? We won our independence from them years ago, just as we will win this war. The great hero of the American

Revolution, General Washington, chose this location for the seat of our government. I say that we should build a new and better city—to honor the memory of our first President. And let the British be hanged!"

Dolly had her way. Within three years, a new Executive Mansion was built where the original structure had stood. Its blackened walls were repainted white to hide all traces of the fire, and it was then that people began to refer to the residence as The White House.

After the signing of the peace treaty in 1815, Dolly returned to her old and cherished role of hostess, but she was now a heroine as well. Throughout the nation, people talked of her bravery and resourcefulness during the war and of her coolness and good judgment. Everyone felt a great debt of gratitude to this gallant First Lady who saved the Declaration of Independence, the portrait of Washington, the invaluable

*. . . no one . . . would have dreamed that she was
the glamorous Dolly Madison . . .*

records of Madison's entire public career, and some silverware as well.

Dolly was still full of gaiety and good fun. A new idea that came to her was that she should help the children of Washington celebrate Easter. So she dyed hundreds of hard-boiled eggs in all colors of the rainbow, and invited the children to an egg-rolling party on the White House lawn. They came in droves, and the event was such a success that it became a national institution—a custom that continues to this very day.

At the end of his second term, James Madison was a tired old man, worn to a shadow by his heavy responsibilities. He retired to the Virginia plantation, and faithfully Dolly gave up the exciting life of the capital to take care of her ailing husband.

After Madison's death, Dolly returned to Washington. Despite her white hair and wrinkles, she was still striking in appearance. She was voted a seat on the floor of the House of Representatives, an honor never before granted to a woman. And she spent these last twelve years of her life glorying in the Washington society that she had reigned over for so long.

During her lifetime, she had seen eleven Presidents come and go. Her great contributions during the important formative years of our republic are political history. Dolly Madison will be remembered as our most popular and most glamorous First Lady.

# SACAJAWEA
## *Indian Guide of the Far West*

MOST PEOPLE have heard about Meriwether Lewis and William Clark, those courageous American explorers who broke through the wilderness and opened up the West. But *few* people know that if it had not been for a little Indian girl, they could never have accomplished their historic feat.

When Lewis and Clark started on their famous journey, they aimed to make their way across the whole United States until they reached the Pacific Ocean. To do this, they had to travel through thousands of miles of wild, unmapped territory. They knew that this country was swarming with savage Indians. They thought it would be a good idea to hire a guide to show them the way—someone who knew where the rivers were, where the mountains were, where the swamps were. A trustworthy guide could give them information about the dangerous Indians, too.

One day, Lewis and Clark came to a little village in Wisconsin. Here they were told that a certain fur trapper would make a good guide. They went directly to the trapper's cabin. However, they soon discovered that the trapper could not help them too much, but his wife could. She was the kind of a guide they had been searching for.

This shy little Indian maid had been born in the territory they planned to explore. She knew the countryside well. She was familiar with the different tribes of Indians that lived there. She also spoke a number of Indian languages. Her name was Sacajawea.

Sacajawea had been carried off from her tribe by Indian enemies when she was nine years old. Later, they sold her to the fur trapper, and she worked for him. As she grew up, she became very pretty. The fur trapper married her.

When Lewis and Clark first met Sacajawea, she was sixteen years old, and already the mother of a newborn baby. And when the explorers asked her and her husband to become their guides, Sacajawea strapped her baby on her back and set forth.

Lewis and Clark felt that they were in luck to get this young couple as their guides. But they didn't know just how lucky they were until they were beset by real troubles. Then it was that the young Indian girl showed her mettle.

Imagine what it must have been like to walk for months, with a heavy pack strapped to your back, through forests full of wild animals. At any moment, an angry beast might spring out of the dense woods to attack.

At any moment, too, the explorers might have been attacked by the hostile Indians.

But in addition to the perils of wild animals and Indians, there was another enemy even more deadly. The forest's greatest danger was starvation.

In those days, there were no canned foods, so there was no way of carrying more than a few days' food supply on any journey. When all the food was gone, it was Sacajawea who saved the party from starving to death by digging up wild roots and cooking them. She taught the explorers how to identify animal tracks, how to find drinking water, what wild plants were poisonous. Time and again, she saved their lives.

It was Sacajawea who found a path through the wilderness. It was Sacajawea who showed courage when even the men quailed with fear. Without her knowledge and wisdom, they would all surely have perished—either killed by wild beasts, wiped out by roving Indian bands, or destroyed by hunger.

This young girl in her teens led the Lewis and Clark expedition through trackless forests, keeping pace with

*It was Sacajawea who found a path
through the wilderness.*

the strongest man. She trudged along as tirelessly as the most rugged among them. She endured hunger and other hardships with never a complaint. In fact, she inspired the whole party by her courage, her cleverness, and her sweetness. Many a cold, dreary night, deep in the forest, surrounded by terrors of all kinds, Sacajawea nourished their bodies with hot food, and soothed their spirits with a sweet song and her calm manner.

But this modest, wise little Indian girl was not only brave and helpful, strong and intelligent; she possessed that rare gift with which only great leaders are blessed —she could think and act quickly in a crisis. Once, when a sudden windstorm capsized their boat, it was she who, quick as a flash, pulled their equipment and food supplies from the water before they were swept away. If she had not acted with such speed, the whole expedition would have had to be abandoned.

One day, after months of journeying, the Lewis and Clark expedition came to the woods where Sacajawea was born. But it was home to her no more. Gone were her people, her family, her loved ones. Mile after mile they traveled, but there was no sign of her tribe.

Suddenly, her friends saw an astonishing thing. Sacajawea was jumping up and down and pointing ahead of them as if she would go mad with joy.

They looked, and saw a small band of Indians approaching. A woman ran forward and clasped Sacajawea in her arms. Sacajawea had found her people! The woman who embraced her so tenderly was her childhood companion. Never in her wildest dreams had Sacajawea expected to see her friend again.

But an even greater surprise was yet to come when her friend led her back to the tribe. For the chief turned out to be none other than Sacajawea's own brother!

This meeting proved to be a wonderful piece of

good fortune. Because of their love for Sacajawea, the Indians gave the Lewis and Clark expedition safe conduct through their country, and also sold the white men some much-needed horses. Without these horses, the expedition could never have made its way across the deserts and over the peaks that lay ahead.

Even though Sacajawea yearned to stay with her people, she did not desert the Lewis and Clark expedition. When the time came to go, she bade her family farewell, and faithfully fulfilled her task as she had promised to do.

It took eight long, harrowing months of struggle through mountains, deserts, swamps, and forests; but at last the great day came when the members of the exhausted little party caught sight of the Pacific Ocean. How their hearts beat with joy and thankfulness!

They had hoped to find trading ships on the coast, but none appeared. Finally, they had to start back on their return journey without the supplies they needed so desperately and which they had counted on getting from the ships. The trip back was shorter, for they had learned the way. But although it took only five months to return, as compared with eight months to get across to the Pacific, they endured worse mishaps and suffered much more than on the outward journey.

At long last, the expedition reached Sacajawea's village once again. They had traveled five thousand miles!

*. . . when the little party caught sight of the
Pacific . . . their hearts beat with joy . . .!*

What a store of important information they brought back with them! The knowledge gained by this handful of courageous men, aided by an extraordinary teenage girl, gave pioneer families the confidence they needed to settle the vast lands of the West. It is because of pathfinders like Meriwether Lewis and William Clark, and the noble Indian girl, Sacajawea, that America became the great and wonderful country it is today.

# MARY LYON
## *Trailblazer in Education*

WHEN MARY LYON was born back in 1797, it was foolish to think of a girl going to school after she was ten years old.

"Ridiculous!" people said. "Of course, she can use reading and writing, for a good housewife ought to be able to keep her accounts when she goes shopping. But she doesn't have to know any more than that, does she?"

To send a girl to college and give her a *real* education—that was out of the question.

But this old-fashioned way of thinking didn't stop Mary Lyon. "Men think they have all the brains," she said, "but we girls know they haven't. We like to learn things, too."

Mary's father was a poor man. How could he buy her books with which to learn about all the wonderful things in the world?

"I'll find a way, somehow," said Mary.

When she was very young, she got a job as a housekeeper. Her salary was one dollar a week, but Mary's eyes lit up when she got her first week's pay. After her employer handed her the money, she stole quietly into her room and shut the door. Then she knelt down and pulled out a box from under her bed. With a key that she kept on a string around her neck, she opened the box. She put the dollar into it and locked it up again. That night, Mary vowed that she would save every penny she earned to buy books.

It was not long before the thrifty young girl went to the bookseller's and made her first purchase. As she eagerly read the pages, her heart thumped loudly in her chest. She knew that what she wanted to do most in the world was to study.

If only she could go to school! It was good to read books, but Mary wanted teachers to guide her, and to tell her what was best to read. So Mary took on other work. At night, in her spare time, she would do sewing and spinning and weaving. Finally, when she was twenty years old, she had managed to save enough money for one term of school.

Those were glorious months! Studies came easily to her, and her teachers praised her highly. The principal of the school was so taken with Mary's ability that he allowed her to stay in school another term, free of charge. But after that, for lack of funds, she had to leave.

Those two terms in school started Mary thinking about something very important. "How would it be," she thought, "if there were a college just for girls?"

That was it! If men wouldn't allow women to go to their colleges, women would simply have to have a college of their own. "How terribly unfair," Mary said, "for boys to get an education and not girls. Intelligent girls are losing all that is best in life just because they weren't born to wear trousers."

Mary took a job as a teacher in a small school in Ipswich, Massachusetts. Whenever she had a chance, she would tell her idea to ministers, doctors, lawyers —anyone who would listen to her. On vacations and holidays, she traveled long distances to see the presidents of men's colleges.

But they all answered her with the same discouraging question: "When girls become scholars, who is to make our puddings and pies?" Men were more interested in their stomachs than in helping women get an education.

As the years passed, Mary never stopped trying. Though, one by one, all the renowned men of her time refused to help her, Mary did not give up. Even though she hated to beg, her desire to carry her idea through was so great that she went from door to door, asking the women of Ipswich for pennies, dimes, and quarters. At last, she had collected a thousand dollars.

"Now the important men will listen to me," she said, and she went back to them. When they saw what this one courageous woman had done, they were so impressed that they, too, gave her money.

On the morning of October 13, 1836, Mary Lyon stood proudly by as workmen in overalls lowered the first stone into the ground at South Hadley, Massachusetts. It took a year to complete the building, but when it was finished, Mary put a sign above the door reading "Mount Holyoke Seminary For Girls." It was the first woman's college in America.

That year, eighty-five girls were accepted by the college. Three short years later, Mount Holyoke enrolled 250 girls. They came from every state in the Union. Some even traveled across the ocean from foreign lands to get an education at Mary's college.

Her dream had come true! For twelve wonderful years, Mary remained in charge of the school. Then, one night, she was called to nurse a sick student. Mary stayed so close to the poor girl that she herself became ill—and in a few days she died.

Her friends and students were shocked and heartbroken. In the days that followed, they put up a beautiful white marble monument in honor of this admirable woman. They vowed that what Mary Lyon had started

*Mary put a sign above the door . . .*

would never die.

Mount Holyoke College continued to grow through the years, and soon other colleges for women were founded throughout the country. Today, an American girl can get as much education as her heart desires, thanks to the efforts of Mary Lyon, the woman who would not rest until she had made her dream—education for her fellow women—come true.

# DOROTHEA DIX
## Crusader for the Mentally Ill

IT WAS AN icy winter morning. The ground was bare
and frozen. Two women stood in front of an odd little
shed. The smaller woman held two large iron keys in
her hand. As she was about to unlock the door of the
shed, she suddenly stopped. A frightening scream came
from inside.

"You're sure you want to go in there, ma'am?"
asked the woman with the keys.

"Please open the door, Mrs. Stone," the other
woman replied.

Mrs. Stone did as she was told, and the two women
bent down to look inside. There was just enough room
in the shed for a man to lie down. The shed was no
bigger than a large box—only seven feet square! There

were no windows in this little house, so that it was always pitch-black inside. And no fresh air could enter except when the door was opened for a miserable plate of food scraps to be thrust in. The shed had a double door, with two strong locks.

As the light flooded in from the doorway, the screaming stopped. An old man with white hair and bright blue eyes was sitting at the feet of the two women, on the iron-hard dirt floor. His teeth were chattering, and he was shivering with cold. He seemed frightened.

The visitor was startled and horrified to see that the old man was tied by an ox chain that ran from an iron ring in the ground to a similar iron band around his ankle!

"That's him," Mrs. Stone whispered. "He ain't strong enough to do a body harm, but I wouldn't go too close.

Dorothea Dix did go close. She had been going close to people like this old man for years. She crouched down in front of him. "How do you do, Mr. Simmons," she said. "I'm Miss Dix. I've come to talk with you."

The old man pulled his knees up to his chest and pressed himself against the wall.

"He don't understand what you say, ma'am. No use talking to old Abe Simmons, ma'am. I give up talking to him three years ago."

*The visitor was . . . horrified to see that the old
man was tied by an ox chain . . .*

"You must be very cold and lonely in here," Dorothea said to the old man. It was peculiar the way she spoke, almost like a mother talking to a child. The old man didn't answer.

"Don't worry about that, ma'am," Mrs. Stone said from the doorway. "Old Abe don't know the difference. To tell you the honest truth, I don't think he even knows where he is most of the time." Mrs. Stone chuckled a little.

Dorothea reached out and took one of the old man's hands in hers. He didn't draw away, but let her hold it. "Why, your hand is icy, Mr. Simmons," she said, rubbing briskly to warm it. "Don't you ever have a stove in here with you?"

"You know, ma'am," Mrs. Stone said, "sometimes my husband comes in here and cleans out an inch of frost. Be enough to kill an ordinary human, but old Abe's tough as a rock. Hangs on year after year. My husband says crazy people ain't like the rest of us. Don't need no comforts, 'cause they're dreaming all the time, he says."

"Would you like me to send you some blankets, Mr. Simmons?" Dorothea asked. "And a bed to sleep on at night?"

The old man, who had been staring at Dorothea with no expression on his face other than the fear in his bright blue eyes, nodded his head. A tear slid down his cheek.

"Land o' Goshen," Mrs. Stone said in surprise. "I think he understood what you were saying, ma'am."

"Of course he did." Dorothea Dix stood up. "Mrs. Stone, where do you and your husband keep your cows and chickens in the winter?"

"Why, in the barn, ma'am, like everybody else," Mrs. Stone said.

"And is it warm in the barn?"

"Yes, ma'am. The critters keep the barn warm with their own bodies. Everyone knows that."

"Do you think Abraham Simmons deserves as good treatment as your cows, Mrs. Stone?" Dorothea spoke firmly.

"Well, I don't know ma'am. I never thought of it that way. Old Abe, here, is different from a cow or a chicken."

Dorothea led her companion out into the fresh air again. "Yes," she said, "he *is* different. He's a human being. And something must be done about him!

"Tell me, Mrs. Stone," she continued, as they left the old man, "why do you have the double door and the two locks? Surely, Mr. Simmons is so feeble that such precautions are unnecessary."

"Oh, sometimes he screams dreadfully," Mrs. Stone answered. "The noise disturbed us in the house, so Mr. Stone put the second door on. It makes it quieter."

Dorothea Dix, who spent her life trying to improve the lot of the mentally ill, had traveled all over her home state of Massachusetts, and everywhere she had met the same attitude. In some towns, men and women like old Abe Simmons were kept in jails along with criminals. In smaller villages like Mrs. Stone's, where there were no jails, the "crackpots," the lunatics, and the "tetched in the head," like Abe, were boarded out to families.

Actually, they were auctioned off like cattle, except that they went to the lowest bidder instead of the highest. The towns had to pay for their support, and they wanted it to be as cheap as possible. Since the families who took them were trying to make a profit on these unhappy people, they naturally spent as little as they could on comforts and food for their charges.

As a result, Dorothea, in going from town to town, would find these unfortunates locked in attics or chained to walls in cellars. Almost always, they were underfed and poorly clothed. Sometimes they were on the verge of starvation, like old Abe.

Dorothea found that often it was not meanness or cruelty that made people treat these unfortunates in this fashion; it was ignorance. Like Mrs. Stone and her husband, people felt that because these *loonies* couldn't complain about their troubles, because sometimes they screamed and acted queerly, these crazy ones didn't know the difference between warmth and cold, between hunger and being well-fed.

People would say that they were dangerous and had

to be put away for safety's sake. But Dorothea found hundreds of feeble-minded men and women who were not really insane, but simply not intelligent enough to take care of themselves. Even these would be locked in airless closets or jammed into prison cells so tightly that they would hardly have room to lie down on the floor at night.

Dorothea found that almost none of the mentally sick people were ever cured. Wherever they happened to be put when they became ill, there they stayed until they died.

Dorothea visited every hospital, prison, and insane asylum that she could find in the state, and then she wrote a report for the Governor of Massachusetts. He could hardly believe what he read, but he investigated and found that every word was true. As a result, laws were passed, and money was allotted to improve the shameful conditions.

But Dorothea was not content with that. In 1843, she began to travel through other parts of the United States, investigating mistreatment of the mentally sick. In those days, voyaging was no easy matter. Trains were few, and they were nothing like the ones we have today. There were no sleeping cars, so anyone traveling a long distance had to sit up all the way. The coaches were heated with little stoves, which made them stifling hot for those in the nearest seats and uncomfortably chilly for the passengers farther away.

But they were the least of the discomforts of travel. Many places could be reached only by stage or lumber wagon. There were so many breakdowns that Dorothea got into the habit of carrying with her a small kit containing carpenter's tools, nails, rope, leather for patching harnesses, and a can of axle grease.

Despite all these difficulties, Dorothea traveled 60,000 miles—enough to take her across our country twenty times! Before long, she had become so well known for her good deeds that railroad companies had begun sending her free tickets so that she might go wherever she was needed.

When the Civil War broke out, Dorothea gave up, for a time, her work for the mentally ill. She offered the services of herself and some other nurses to give free care to wounded soldiers. Her offer was accepted and she was given a commission as Superintendent of United States Army Nurses—the first commission of its kind ever issued.

After the war was over, she went back to her original vocation. Because of her investigations, hospitals for mental patients were built in thirty-six states. And they were staffed with doctors and nurses —not jailers or ignorant people like Mrs. Stone and her husband.

Today, the United States has more facilities to care for the mentally ill than any other country in the world.

*. . . jammed into prison cells so tightly that they*
*would hardly have room to lie down . . .*

Only a short while ago, another nation-wide inquiry was carried out to see what was being done for men and women like Abraham Simmons. In some parts of the country, especially in the more backward states, hospitals for the mentally ill were found to be old, over-crowded, poorly equipped and maintained. Books and articles were written about these conditions. People immediately became interested, just as they had when Dorothea Dix exposed her findings. Money was raised, doctors were employed, and new buildings were constructed for these sick people.

It is because people have a way of forgetting the mentally ill, once they are hospitalized, that these abuses can happen.

We realize today that there is no evil or shame connected with mental disorders. Just as a man can have trouble with his heart or his lungs or his liver, his brain can become ill. Dorothea Dix showed us that the mentally sick are not possessed of devils; they don't need chains, jails, and jailers.

Dorothea Dix proved that with care and kindness, science can cure many people who may seem to most of us to be hopelessly insane.

# HARRIET BEECHER STOWE
## *Fighter Against Slavery*

"YOU'LL NEVER run away from me again, you no-account swine. This is the fourth time and the *last* time. I'm going to beat you till you can't even move, much less run!"

It was a white man speaking. Beside him stood two big, strong Negro slaves. Kneeling before them on the dirt floor of a tumble-down shack was an old gray-haired Negro man.

Tears were streaming down the old man's cheeks. He was pleading for mercy. "Please, massah, don't beat me. Ah'll never run away again. Ah learned mah lesson. Ah'll never do it again."

The white man's cruel voice broke with anger. He turned to the two young Negroes who stood beside him. "Lay the whips to that slave," he shouted.

The two young Negroes didn't move. They looked down at the ground.

"You heard me, you miserable dogs. Put the whip to him." The white man's face turned red with anger.

Still, the Negroes didn't move.

The white man drew a pistol from his belt and cocked the hammer. "You men are my property. And you'll do as I say, by God, or I'll shoot you on the spot. Now, whip him. And whip him good."

The two Negroes slowly took the heavy blacksnake whips from hooks on the wall. They drew them back and brought them down with a crack across the bare back of the old kneeling slave. His cries of pain and torment were weak and pitiful.

"Harder, harder," the white man shouted. "Teach him what happens to slaves who run away from me."

The two young Negroes brought the big black whips down even more fiercely. Finally, the old gray-haired slave slumped to the floor, unconscious. Only then did the white man tell them to stop.

This horrible incident was brought home to the people of a little Ohio town one Sunday morning a little more than a hundred years ago. As the Reverend Lakestone told the story in all its cruelty, Harriet Beecher Stowe shivered in her seat. To think that she was sitting in a bright, sun-flooded little church, with everything around her beautiful and peaceful, and that such a terrible outrage could occur only a few short miles away!

The preacher had been talking to his congregation about slavery. "My friends, in these troubled times we are all faced with a terrible problem, the question of whether men shall hold other men as slaves. This problem may lead our great nation to war. I want you to pray to God that He will help us find a peaceful solution."

The people in the church bowed their heads. They knew all about the slavery practiced in the Southern states. Just across the river in neighboring Kentucky, all the plantation owners had slaves. And in their own Ohio newspapers, people would often read descriptions of escaped Negroes. Such descriptions might end with: "Ran away from his master, Richard Knewles, Hill Farms, Kentucky. If seen, please notify. REWARD."

The other churchgoing people prayed as the preacher asked, but Harriet Beecher Stowe had seen, in her mind's eye, the terrible beating of the old Negro. Her eyes overflowed with tears, and her heart was torn with pity.

Only the day before, a great crowd had gathered on the river's edge not far from Harriet's house. A slave trader was auctioning 150 Negroes who had recently been shipped over from Africa. She vividly remembered the frightened faces of the men and women and children. But, especially, she recalled one husband and wife who were put up for sale.

"Now what am I offered, ladies and gentlemen?" the auctioneer had shouted. "Here's a good, strong, husky couple of blacks for some lucky buyer. What am I

*They . . . brought the whips down . . . across the
back of the old kneeling slave.*

offered?"

"I'll take the woman for fifty dollars," called a man named Reynolds.

"What do you offer for the *couple,* Mr. Reynolds?" the auctioneer asked.

"'Got all the *men* slaves I need right now," Reynolds answered.

"I'll give sixty for the buck," another buyer said. "I got all the women I can use."

The husband and wife on the platform clung together. Each was all the other had in this strange land.

"I'm offered fifty for the female and sixty for the buck. Do I hear another bid? Do I hear any more? Going . . . Going . . ." The auctioneer raised his wooden hammer. "Gone." He brought it down on the block with a bang. The husband and his wife were sold to separate masters. They would probably never see each other again, for the rest of their lives.

Harriet had stood there while the auctioneer and the new owners tore the Negro man and woman from each other's arms. It was one of the most terrible sights she had ever seen. It made her sick and angry. It made her want to do something to abolish slavery forever.

And after she had heard the preacher in church, Harriet knew exactly what she *could* do. She could go home, sit down at her desk, and write a book to tell the world, the whole world, how unfair and inhuman slavery really was.

She wrote a story about an old colored slave named Uncle Tom, a little black girl called Topsy, and a mean, evil overseer, Simon Legree.

She called the book *Uncle Tom's Cabin*. Soon after it was published, she became famous. Everybody read it, both Northerners and Southerners. In time, it was translated into over twenty foreign languages so that the people in Europe and Asia, Africa and South America could read it, too.

But here in America, bitter arguments arose over the book. Some people in the South, who owned slaves and wanted to keep slavery, called Harriet Beecher Stowe a liar. Others, who realized she had done humanity a priceless service, called her a heroine.

She became so famous that after the Civil War had begun and she was introduced to President Abraham Lincoln, he said to her, "Is this the little woman whose book made such a great war?"

Harriet did not rest. She wrote many other books, many articles and stories against slavery which were printed in magazines and newspapers the world over.

Harriet even played a part in the Underground Railroad. The Underground Railroad consisted of people who had joined together before the Civil War to help slaves get safely away from their Southern masters. Harriet would open her door at night to find a breathless slave standing on the doorstep. She would welcome him, feed him, and give him a safe place to sleep. Then, the

Sale to c
male 28 yrs. hea
male 14
male 55 skill
male 22 gr
female 18 c
female 19 hea

*It was one of the most terrible sights
she had ever seen.*

next night, under cover of darkness, she would send him on to the house of another member of the Underground Railroad. Soon, the escaped slave would be far to the North and free for the rest of his life.

Americans today can thank Harriet Beecher Stowe for dramatizing to America and the world the fact that so dreadful a custom as buying and selling human beings should not be practiced in the land of the free. Perhaps more than any other single person, this gallant little lady was responsible for the abolition of slavery in the United States.

# IDAWALLEY LEWIS
## *Dauntless Rescuer at Sea*

IT WAS A black, scowling day. A terrible, howling storm was raging in Newport Harbor. The water was wild! Heavy rollers crashed against the walls of the lighthouse.

Inside, Ida Lewis lay on her bed. She was suffering from a severe cold. Her bed had been placed next to the kitchen oven, and she lay bundled in towels and blankets. She stirred fitfully now and then, exhausted from her fever.

Suddenly, above the roar of the tempest, she heard a fearful cry. Thrusting the coverings from her, she sprang to her desk, quickly grabbed a telescope from the drawer, clapped it to her eye, and gazed out to sea. Her eye could scarcely pierce the leaping spray.

Half a minute later, she put down the glass, and ran to the closet for her sou'wester.

"Ida!" her mother cried. "You can't go out in this storm in your condition. You'll get pneumonia. And anyhow, not even a healthy person could stay afloat in this weather."

"There are men out there who need help. I must get to them! I cannot think of myself now!"

And so, in spite of the pleadings of her mother, Ida went out into the storm.

Rowing against that fearful tide taxed every ounce of Ida's strength. She had to fight her sickness *and* the sea. At last, she reached the capsized boat. Nearby, two exhausted soldiers were struggling in the water. With the salt spray stinging her eyes, and the raging sea bouncing her small craft about, she grasped one of the men. Though her illness had left her very weak, her will power seemed to force new strength into her young arms. Gradually, Ida drew the half-drowned, helpless soldiers into her skiff.

The trip back to the lighthouse proved even more difficult. Now Ida had to row with the added weight of two heavy men, against the buffetings of the sea. But unaided, she brought the boat to safety.

Where did Ida Lewis get such courage and strength? And where did she get the skill to be able to perform such a heroic act? Did she come from a family of fisherfolk brought up amidst the perils of the sea?

Had she, from childhood, learned how to handle heavy boats against a heavy tide?

The answer to all these questions is "No." When Ida was a girl of fifteen, her father, Hosea Lewis, had come home to his family to make the startling announcement: "I have been made the keeper of the Lime Rock Lighthouse."

"What of the children?" Mrs. Lewis had asked. "They have always lived here in Newport. They go to school here. How can we take them out to that bleak rock in the harbor?"

It was a difficult decision for the family to make. But they moved into the lighthouse. To fifteen-year-old Ida, a whole new world was being opened. She knew nothing of boats or of the sea.

Shortly afterward, Mr. Lewis suffered a paralytic stroke and became a hopeless invalid. Mrs. Lewis was desperate. She now had a sick husband and four children to support. The running of the lighthouse seemed a task too great for her, and she wanted to leave.

"We cannot abandon the lighthouse," pleaded young Ida. "Too many people depend on us for their safety. This great beacon must be kept burning so that the ships can find their way."

"But we cannot undertake such a job. The children are too small to help, and we, after all, are only two women," argued her mother.

But Ida Lewis was not frightened.

"You can take care of the light, trimming the wick and feeding it with oil. I will row the children to and from school and bring the supplies from the mainland," said young Ida.

She was true to her word. Although she had never rowed before, she took the boat out daily for practice, fair weather or foul.

It was not until two years later that Ida's selfless courage was revealed. One September afternoon, she was watching a catboat in the harbor when a sudden squall overturned it. Without a moment's hesitation, she dashed to her skiff and rowed to the rescue of the passengers.

"Hang on. Don't give up," she cried. "I'll save you!"

Mustering all her frail strength, she pulled four young men into her small craft.

This was the beginning of a career of rescues and self-sacrifice unequaled in the annals of the sea. Ida had ten rescues to her credit when, in 1869, she rescued the two soldiers. She became a national heroine.

In token of their homage, the people of her home town, Newport, gave her a beautiful new boat, *The Rescue*. But Ida's fame spread beyond her native state of Rhode Island. Everywhere, her bravery was paid the highest praise. She remained modest in spite of these honors, stating simply, "I just did my duty. That's all there was to it."

*. . . Ida drew the half-drowned, helpless soldiers
into her skiff.*

# MARIA MITCHELL
## *Great Woman Astronomer*

NANTUCKET is a unique American town. Located on an island in the Atlantic Ocean, off the coast of Massachusetts, it was one of the great centers of the whaling industry during the nineteenth century. Most of the menfolk of the town—from the age of fourteen to seventy—went off on long voyages in search of whales, voyages that sometimes lasted as much as three years. The women were left behind to do the jobs that in any other place would have been handled by the men. This curious situation produced a breed of fearless and independent women—capable, self-reliant, and sure of themselves and their opinions.

It also produced a woman unique in the annals of American history. Great women scientists are rare enough anywhere in the world. But it was in Nantucket that a girl grew up who became an internationally famous astronomer. Her name was Maria Mitchell.

Maria showed an unusual talent from an early age: she loved mathematics. Not only did she love to do her arithmetic homework and study over her figures for hours; she was fascinated by a very special branch of mathematics, and in this she was strongly influenced by her father. He was interested in the heavenly bodies —the stars, comets, and planets—and in their magnitude, motions, and composition. He had a small telescope on the roof of their house, through which he gazed at the heavens for hours on end. And Maria soon joined him in this study of *astronomy*.

It was natural that when Maria grew to be a young lady, she should remain in her island home and serve as a schoolteacher there. Though a disciplinarian, she had natural charm and an obvious love of knowledge that endeared her to her pupils and helped her to teach them their lessons well.

Maria also continued her telescope observations and began to compile an exhaustive set of notes on what she was learning about planets and space. She had heard that the King of Denmark was offering a gold medal to the first person who discovered a new heavenly body by telescope. Because Maria considered herself only an amateur astronomer, she had little hope of winning such an award. But her eyes, searching through the telescope lens, continued to sweep the skies night after night—and she hoped that somehow all her work might produce something important.

On the evening of October 1, 1847, there was a party in the Mitchell household. Friends and neighbors were gathered for a pleasant evening of talk and refreshments. The fall winds were beginning to sweep in from the ocean and across the island, and it was good to be in the cozy, snug Mitchell parlor. Maria enjoyed the company of these people, but neither they nor the weather could force her to give up even one night at her telescope on the roof. So, at an opportune moment, she excused herself for some trivial reason and was off to her stargazing.

Some time later, she returned to the party, but only long enough to whisper a message to her father: "You must come to the roof, Father. I think I've seen a new comet."

When he followed her to the roof, she pointed out the comet to him. Skeptical at first, he soon let his scientific curiosity get the best of him, and he took up the telescope. A few minutes later, he broke forth with an exclamation of excitement: "By Jupiter, Maria, you're right! Do you realize what this means? This is an entirely new comet that no one has ever seen before. You've made a historic discovery. We must send the news off to Harvard University at once."

And so they did. Meanwhile, only two days later,

an Englishman observed the very same comet; several other people followed suit shortly afterward. But Maria Mitchell had been the first; there was no disputing that fact.

For her discovery of this comet, observed through a small brass telescope with only a three-inch lens, Maria Mitchell was awarded the gold medal by the King of Denmark. No other woman had ever made such an important discovery in the history of astronomy, and she became famous overnight. She was honored as the first woman to be elected a Fellow of the American Academy of Arts and Sciences, though the finicky old secretary of that organization erased the word fellow and substituted honorary member. This unjust act made Maria Mitchell a militant champion of equal rights for women in the years to come.

For the next twenty years, Maria Mitchell served as librarian in Nantucket and continued her astronomical studies of sunspots, satellites, nebulae, and such things. This strong, resourceful woman, who also had a delightful sense of humor, was popular with the boys preparing to go off on their first whaling cruises. She often applied her mathematical skills to helping them learn the use of the *sextant,* the instrument used at sea for measuring distances.

During this time, Maria also made a trip to Europe, and was received with great honor wherever she went, for her reputation had been growing for a long time.

*. . . she pointed out the comet to him.*

She met and talked with the most famous astronomers and mathematicians of the Old World, impressing everyone with her remarkable knowledge.

The new women's college, Vassar, had been founded in 1861, and it was appropriate that Maria Mitchell was appointed as its first Professor of Astronomy. At first she had refused, feeling that her lack of experience in college teaching would handicap her. But the authorities prevailed upon her, and she served at Vassar with great distinction for twenty-three years. The figure of this tall, majestic woman with the tight, iron-gray curls tucked under her black bonnet became a familiar and loved one on the campus of Vassar. The force of her personality and her great skill as an astronomer made her a first-rate teacher. And she also continued her research work, studying the planets Jupiter and Saturn and doing pioneer work with photography of the sun.

There are several amusing anecdotes connected with her stay at Vassar. Once, as she was walking across the campus, a student called to her: "Professor Mitchell, I beg your pardon, but there's a hole in your stocking." Maria turned to the proper young girl and retorted coolly, "What, is there only *one*?"

Another of her students drew attention to the professor's shawl which was trailing on the ground. Not caring to be bothered with such insignificant matters— or, perhaps, indulging in a sly jest—Maria answered, "Oh, yes, I prefer it that way."

When she died in 1889, Maria Mitchell had carried off more degrees and honors than any other woman of her generation. A sculptured figure of her was unveiled in the New York University Hall of Fame in 1922—a fitting salute to a woman who had defied tradition to become a great astronomer.

# HARRIET TUBMAN
## *Moses of the Negro People*

NIGHTTIME ON A Southern plantation . . . flickering darts of flame among the trees . . . the light of a campfire . . . soft voices singing, "When the old chariot comes, I'm going to leave you, going to cross over to the promised land."

It is a group of Negro slaves worn out after the day's hard labor.

The sound of the singing rises and falls gently in the evening stillness. Suddenly, a figure appears in the shadows. A short, heavy man walks toward the campfire, his finger on his lips to command silence. The song stops.

"It's Moses!" one slave whispers. "Glory be to God, it's Moses come to save us!"

But this deliverer is not a man at all. It is Harriet Tubman, come to lead more of her people to freedom.

In a moment, the campfire site is empty. In the little slave cabins, there are quick, hurried movements, low voices. Bundles are being made. An old coat, a blanket, some scraps of food are hastily tied together. A baby is tucked into a basket. In a moment, the cabins will be empty. The slaves will be on their way north, to freedom!

And who will lead them on their long, dangerous journey? Who will show them what paths to take, tell them when it is safe to travel and when they must hide? Who will know in what houses live people ready to give them food and a place to sleep? Who will show them at just what bend in the river there is a boat waiting to speed them many miles north? Who will calm the fearful, command the rebellious, and keep the little group of runaway slaves together and full of courage on their escape route? Harriet Tubman, the general without an army, the woman whom her people call Moses, a runaway slave with a price of $40,000 on her head. *Harriet Tubman will lead her enslaved people to freedom.*

For Harriet Tubman knew the meaning of slavery. Her owner had made her work before she was five years old. Her mistress beat her every day. She had seen fellow slaves separated from their families, fathers torn away from their children, human beings sold to another master far away, never to see their loved ones again.

When she was fourteen, she was sent to labor in the fields. She worked all day long with no rest, with the hot sun beating down on her from sunrise to sunset, doing the work of a grown man! She knew the fearful history of her people, the dreadful story of how they had been kidnaped from their homes and friends in Africa, packed into the dark, airless holds of ships—packed so tightly that they were unable to move—chained to their seats, and taken far across the ocean to America. Many had died during their journey—of starvation, suffocation, or mistreatment. Those who lived were sold, like work-animals, doomed to spend the rest of their lives in slavery!

Harriet Tubman knew the meaning of freedom, too. All her life, from her childhood on, she had yearned for it, longed for it, dreamed of it. Finally, when she could bear her life as a slave no longer, she had run away. No one had helped her, no one had told her what to do, no one had guided her as she was to lead other runaway, escaping slaves later on. Toward the end of her journey, she met some people who aided her in her escape to the North.

How did Harriet feel when she found that she was free, when she found herself in the North? She said, "When I found I had crossed that line, I looked at my hands to see if I was the same person. There was such a glory over everything. The sun came out like gold through the trees, and I felt as though I was in heaven."

*. . . they had been kidnaped . . . and packed into
the dark, airless holds of ships . . .*

But she could not enjoy her freedom for long, knowing that so many of her people were still enslaved. "I had seen their tears and sighs, and I had heard their groans, and I would give every drop of blood in my veins to free them." So Harriet became a "conductor" on the Underground Railroad. Nineteen times she went back into the South, rescuing three hundred slaves!

The Underground Railroad was not an ordinary railway at all, but a system of roads and paths connecting the homes of slavery-hating people, persons who were sympathetic to runaway slaves and helped them to escape.

It wasn't long before Harriet became known and feared by the Southern plantation owners. Many of them believed she was a man, because they could not credit a woman with as much courage and daring as she had shown. Rewards offered for her capture were increased. Her picture was posted in all the public places of the Southern towns. Parties of armed men were sent out to watch for her. Every moment that she was in the South, her life was in terrible danger. Yet she returned again and again, although she knew that if she were caught, she would be put to death.

"There are two things I've got a right to," she said, "and these are death and liberty. One or the other I mean to have! No one will take me back alive. I shall fight for my liberty, and when the time has come for me to go, the Lord will let them kill me."

But she must have been doing the Lord's work, for she lived to be ninety-three years old. She died in 1913, just fifty years after President Abraham Lincoln had set the slaves free. After her death, the people of Auburn, New York, the town where she had lived, held a great mass meeting in her honor. They put up a bronze tablet in her memory, on the city courthouse, where it stands to this day. It pays tribute to one of the most fearless and whole-hearted fighters for freedom the world has ever seen.

# SUSAN B. ANTHONY
## Champion of Women's Rights

"WHAT THE BLAZES are you doing here?" shouted the man at the big desk. "You women go about your business. Go home and wash the dishes. And if you don't clear out of here fast, I'll get the cops to put you out!"

Everybody in the store stopped and listened. Some of the men just turned around and sneered. Others looked at the fifteen women mockingly and guffawed. One man piped, "Beat it, youse dames. Your kids are dirty." And at that, every man in the place bellowed with laughter.

But this cruel banter didn't faze the tall, stately woman who stood with a piece of paper in her hand at the head of the fourteen other ladies. She didn't budge an inch.

"I've come here to vote for the President of the United States," she said. "He will be my President as well as yours. We are the women who bear the children who will defend this country. We are the women who make your homes, who bake your bread, who rear your sons and give you daughters. We women are citizens of this country just as much as you are, and we insist on voting for the man who is to be the leader of our government."

Her words rang out with the clearness of a bell, and they struck to the heart. No man in the place dared touch her now. The big man at the desk who had threatened her was turned to stone. And then, in silence and with dignity, Susan B. Anthony strode up to the ballot box and dropped into it the paper bearing her vote. Each of the fourteen other women did the same, while every man in the room stood by silently and watched.

It was the year 1872. Too long now had women been denied the rights that should naturally be theirs. Too long now had they endured the injustice of unfair laws—laws that made them mere possessions of men.

Women could earn money, but they might not own it. If a woman was married and went to work, every penny she earned became the property of her husband. In 1872, a man was considered complete master of the household. His wife was taken to be incapable of managing her own affairs. She was supposed to be a nitwit unable to think clearly, and therefore the law mercifully protected her by appointing a guardian—a male guardian, of course—over any property that she was lucky enough to possess.

Women like Susan Anthony writhed at this injustice. Susan saw no reason why her sex should be discriminated against. "Why should only men make the laws?" she cried. "Why should men forge the chains that bind us down? No!" she exclaimed. "It is up to us women to fight for our rights." And she vowed that she would carry on an everlasting battle, as long as the Lord gave her strength, to see that women were made equal in the eyes of the law.

And fight she did. Susan B. Anthony was America's greatest champion of women's rights. She traveled unceasingly from one end of the country to the other. She made thousands of speeches, pleading with men, and trying to arouse women to fight for their rights. She wrote hundreds of pamphlets and letters of protest. It was a bitter and difficult struggle that she entered upon, for the people who opposed her did not hesitate to say all kinds of ugly and untrue things about her and her followers. "No decent woman would talk like that. No refined lady would force her way before judges and men's associations and insist on talking. She is vulgar!"

Many women who knew that Susan Anthony was

*". . . if you don't clear out . . . I'll get the*
*cops to put you out!"*

a refined, intelligent, and courageous woman were afraid to say so. They were afraid that *they* would be looked down on. But in time, they grew to love her for trying to help them.

After a while, more and more housewives gained courage from her example. Then, at crowded meetings, they joined her by the thousands. Many a man began to change his notions when his wife, inspired by Susan B. Anthony, made him feel ashamed at the unfair treatment accorded women. Slowly, the persevering Susan B. Anthony was undermining the fierce stubbornness of men.

On that important day in 1872, she and her faithful followers cast their first ballots for President. But though the men in the polling place were momentarily moved, their minds were not yet opened. In a few days, Susan was arrested and brought before a judge, accused of having illegally entered a voting booth.

"How do you plead?" asked the judge.

"Guilty!" cried Susan. "Guilty of trying to uproot the slavery in which you men have placed us women. Guilty of trying to make you see that we mothers are as important to this country as are the men. Guilty of trying to lift the standard of womanhood, so that men may look with pride upon their wives' awareness of public affairs."

And then, before the judge could recover from this onslaught, she added, "But, Your Honor, *not* guilty of acting against the Constitution of the United States, which says that no person is to be deprived of equal rights under the law. Equal rights!" she thundered. "How can it be said that we women have equal rights, when it is you and you alone who take upon yourselves the right to make the laws, the right to choose your representatives, the right to send only sons on to higher education. You, you blind men, have become slave-holders of your own mothers and wives."

The judge was taken aback. Never before had he heard these ideas expressed to him in such a forceful manner. However, the law was the law! The judge spoke quietly, and without much conviction. "I am forced to fine you one hundred dollars," he said.

"I will not pay it!" declared Susan Anthony. "Mark my words, the law will be changed!" And with that, she strode from the court.

"Shall I follow her and bring her back?" the court clerk asked the judge.

"No, let her go," answered the elderly judge. "I fear that she is right, and that the law will soon be changed."

And Susan did go on, on to further crusades, on across the vast stretches of the United States, proclaiming in every hamlet where her feet trod, her plea for women's rights.

Today, voting by women is an established right. Women may keep what they earn and, whether mar-

*"How do you plead?" asked the judge.
"Guilty!" cried Susan.*

ried or single, own their own property. It is taken for
granted that a woman may go to college and work in
any business or profession she cares to choose. But
these rights, enjoyed by the women of today, were
secured through the valiant efforts of many fighters for
women's freedom, such as the great Susan B. Anthony.

# ELIZABETH BLACKWELL
## *America's First Woman Doctor*

THE SHINY BLADE of Tommy Benson's sharp new
hatchet cut with a satisfying thwack through the piece
of stovewood. He really didn't mind splitting kindling
now that he had a beautiful new tool.

His little sister, Lucy, crowded up close to him to
watch.

"You'd better stand back, Lucy," Tommy said cross-
ly. "I've told you that four times now. You're going to
get hurt if you don't keep out of the way."

Lucy moved back a step. But presently, her curiosity got the better of her and she edged forward
again. Just as the hatchet started down again, her little
hand darted out "to help hold the stick."

There was a horrifying spurt of blood! Tommy

screamed! Mrs. Benson flew from the kitchen door. Women rushed from the neighboring backyards to see what had happened.

"Quick! Run for Dr. Williams, Tommy! Hurry!" Mrs. Benson called out.

"No use going for Dr. Williams," one of the women said. "He's sick in bed with grippe. He can't even stand on his feet."

"But we must get a doctor!" cried Mrs. Benson. "And there's not another one for blocks and blocks. Oh, what can we do? What can we do?" she wailed desperately.

"There's that Miss Blackwell who calls herself a doctor," put in another woman. "She don't have many patients because no one wants a woman doctor. But maybe she's better than nothin'!"

"Run for her, Tommy. Run fast!" called Mrs. Benson.

And so Elizabeth Blackwell got another paying patient. And little Lucy Benson got the expert medical attention she needed—just in the nick of time.

When Elizabeth was a girl, in the 1830's, there were no women doctors at all. Elizabeth thought a woman could understand the ills and problems of other women better than a male doctor could. She was determined to prove that.

But no medical school would take her. Wherever she applied, she always got the same answer—"*No women admitted!"*

So she began to study medicine by herself, reading everything she could lay her hands on. She left her home in Cincinnati, Ohio, to teach at a school in North Carolina, because the principal of the school had been a doctor, and had agreed to teach her some medicine. But even her best friends laughed at her. "That Elizabeth!" they said. "So stubborn and so foolish. Just imagine! She wants to be—of all things—a woman doctor!"

But Elizabeth carried on. After she had learned all she could from the doctor in North Carolina, she persuaded another doctor in South Carolina to let her watch the way he treated his patients. She studied with him for a while, supporting herself by giving music lessons at a nearby boarding school. Elizabeth worked and Elizabeth studied. During these years, she carried on a relentless fight to be admitted to an accredited medical school. And then, when hope seemed almost gone, her efforts were finally rewarded. The Geneva Medical School in Geneva, New York, accepted her as a student.

And now Elizabeth—the only woman in a class of 150 men—had to put up with the jeers of her fellow students. "She's a bold one," they said. "Imagine a woman thinking she can be a doctor!" But despite insult and ridicule, Elizabeth carried on.

In 1849, she received her diploma, thus becoming the first woman doctor in the United States.

*Elizabeth . . . had to put up with the jeers of
her fellow students.*

Then Elizabeth went to Paris and found employment in a French hospital. The French doctors were absolutely amazed by her success with some of the women patients. Finally, her perseverance and study had been rewarded. For the first time, she enjoyed the intense pleasure that comes from recognition.

One of her patients was a baby with sore eyes. It was a difficult case. Elizabeth did what she could for the child, but the baby was not cured.

One night, Elizabeth noticed she couldn't see as well as usual. She rubbed her eyes wearily, and reached out to turn the oil lamp higher. Still, the print of the book she was reading remained blurred. "I guess I've just studied too long," she thought. "I'll go to bed."

But the next day her eyes were no better. Elizabeth had contracted an eye disease from her baby patient. She became blind in one eye.

Yet Elizabeth wouldn't give up her medical career.

When Elizabeth returned to New York and opened her own office in 1851, her problems were not yet over. Other physicians, fearing that the entrance of women into the medical profession would only offer them more competition, refused either to recognize or help her. What was worse, no one who was sick thought of calling *her*. No one had ever heard of a *woman* doctor. They couldn't believe that she could possibly be as competent as a man.

From time to time—through chance, emergency, or

accident—she got a patient. For the first few years, she had but a handful of visitors. People thought it just wasn't decent for a woman to be a doctor. Only when an emergency, like that of Lucy Benson, *forced* people to use her knowledge were her services requested.

Elizabeth's sister, Emily, had decided that she, too, would become a doctor. The path was much easier for her. Elizabeth already had proved that a woman could actually learn medicine. When Emily received her diploma, the two sisters opened a small infirmary. This later became the New York Infirmary and College for Women. The little hospital they started is now one of the largest training grounds for women doctors in the whole world.

Because of the courage and never-say-die spirit of Elizabeth Blackwell, there are now thousands of women doctors serving humanity all over the face of the globe.

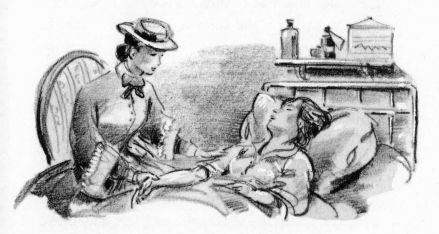

# CLARA BARTON
## *Founder of the American Red Cross*

WHEN THE agonizing pain receded a bit, Jack Gibbs was able to think again. "I'll never make it home," he groaned. "Not in one piece, anyway."

He sighed and tried to shift his body to a more comfortable position on the cold, rocky ground. But the movement caused another warm gush, and he knew that if he were to live at all, he must lie still.

"By the time they cart me back to the hospital behind the lines," he thought, "I'll either have bled to death or I'll be in such rotten shape, they'll have to take my leg off. And what kind of a husband would I be for Sue? A man with one leg!"

A black cloud swept over him, and he lay unconscious. When he opened his eyes again, Jack was sure he had

died and gone to heaven. A woman was bending over
him. That just couldn't happen on a battlefield of the
Civil War. No woman ever came on the field. No woman
would want to! *No woman would be allowed to!*

But there *was* a woman on the battlefield. She was
Clara Barton.

With the help of two soldiers, she lifted Jack onto a
cot which the men had removed from a horse-drawn van.
She took some bandages out of her kit and bound up his
leg. Then she gave him a pain-killing drink. Jack weakly
sipped it down, and the men put him in the crude-look-
ing ambulance.

Clara Barton had been doing this kind of work all
day long. She had given succor to hundreds of the
wounded, allayed their fears, relieved their pain,
cleansed their wounds.

Ever since the dreadful war had begun, Clara Barton
had been worried about the men fighting at the front.
She knew that wounded men were left lying on the field
until the battle was over. She knew that only then were
they collected and taken to hospitals—hospitals far behind the lines. She knew that if they survived this delay,
the rough jolting of the wagons might well cause their
unbound wounds to open. She knew that they often bled
to death before they reached the hospital.

Heartsick at this state of affairs, she determined to
bring aid to the men *right on the field*. First, she procured a van. Then she equipped it with medicines and

first-aid supplies. And then, she went to see the General.

She was a slender little woman. To the commanding officer, she didn't look exactly like battlefield material. In fact, her pet idea horrified him.

"Miss Barton," he said, "what you are asking is absolutely impossible."

"But, General," she insisted, "why is it impossible? I myself will drive the van and give the soldiers what relief I can."

The General shook his head. "The battlefield is no place for a woman. You couldn't stand the rough life. Anyway, we are now doing everything that can be done for our soldiers. No one could do more."

"*I* could," Clara Barton declared. And then, as if she had just entered the room for the first time, she described all over again to the General her plans for first aid on the field.

This interview was repeated again and again, but constant refusal did not deter her. Finally, the commanding officer gave in. Clara Barton received a pass that would let her through the lines.

During the entire course of the Civil War, she ministered to all she could reach. She labored unceasingly. Once she worked with scant rest for five days and nights in a row. Her name became a byword in the Army, spoken of with love and gratitude.

As the government saw what she was actually accomplishing, it gradually afforded her more and more cooperation. The Army supplied more vans and more men to drive them. More medical supplies were made available. But it was, nevertheless, an uphill battle all the way for the courageous Miss Barton.

When the war ended, Clara Barton might have been expected to take a well-earned rest. Instead, she was haunted by the thought of the agony of those unfortunate people who did not know for sure what had happened to their husbands, their fathers, their brothers. She determined to find out about these missing soldiers, and to send the information to their families. She worked at this task for a long time.

Now she knew war at first hand. She knew what it did to men on the battlefield, and she knew what it did to the families they left behind. When she heard that there was a man in Switzerland, by the name of Jean Henry Dunant, who had a plan to help soldiers in wartime, she immediately went to Switzerland to lend her aid. Dunant formed an organization called the *Red Cross.* Workers of this organization were to wear a red cross on a white background so that they could easily be identified. They were to be allowed free access to battlefields, so that they might help *all* soldiers, no matter what their nationality, race, or religion.

Here was a project that fired Clara Barton. She came back to America and convinced the United States Government that it should join with the twenty-two

*She labored unceasingly.*

other nations to give money and supplies to an International Red Cross, organized to help soldiers in wartime.

But Clara Barton added another idea to this great Red Cross plan. It was called the *American Amendment.*

"There are many other calamities that befall mankind," she said, "earthquakes, floods, forest fires, epidemics, tornadoes. These disasters strike suddenly, killing and wounding many, leaving others homeless and starving. The Red Cross should stretch out a hand of help to all such victims, no matter where such disasters befall."

Today, the International Red Cross brings succor to millions of people all over the world. This was in large part Clara Barton's wonderful creation. Her admirable courage, love of humanity, and charity to all will ever be revered.

# EMMA LAZARUS
## Champion of Immigrants

THE GREAT three-masted clipper ship, the *Princess Maria,* stood docked in New York Harbor. She had just arrived from Europe after a voyage of thirty days on the high seas. She had encountered raging winds and fierce waves. Most of her sails were furled, but some hung in tatters from the masts.

The first-class passengers paraded down the gangplank. They were richly dressed, and they chattered gaily with each other or waved greetings to friends and relatives who had come to meet them. After them came the second-class passengers, and then the third-class passengers. Most of these people were tourists and businessmen.

A half-hour after these passengers had disembarked

and their baggage had been unloaded, the holds of the ship spewed forth a strange medley of humans: men whose long beards were blacker than their long coats; women wearing sweaters or shawls, many of them carrying infants in their arms; young men with faces unshaved, tense, tired, haggard, worn. Down they came, pouring down the gangplank and off the ship, like so many cattle.

They carried their own baggage, these people did. No porters for them. And what baggage it was! Battered suitcases, odds and ends wrapped in blankets, paper-covered bundles bound with rope and slung over their shoulders. Now and then, one would see a forlorn woman trudging along with five or six children. No father. Alone with her orphans, she hauled along the pitiful packages that constituted the only possessions she had in this world.

As these ragged, frightened immigrants stepped down onto the dock, they were led by men in uniform to a large building nearby. Suddenly, a shrill scream was heard! A little boy, holding on desperately to his mother's bright peasant skirt, began to cry in mortal fear. The woman bent down and spoke gently to him in a strange, foreign tongue. She stroked his head until the lad quieted down.

"What's the trouble here?" one of the men in uniform asked, as he came up to them.

The young boy cowered behind his mother.

"My son, he has fear," the woman said, with a marked accent.

"There is nothing to be frightened of," the man said, moving around to the boy.

"He no understand," the woman answered. "He think you kill us."

The man in uniform laughed. "He does, now. Well, what makes Josef think I would do a thing like that?"

"It was a man in uniform, like you, that kill his father," the woman said. "I tell him this is America. People no kill here. He no understand."

"That's right, my lad," the man said. "No need to jump at everyone who wears a fancy hat." The guard tried to get closer to the boy, but the lad backed away in terror. His mother whispered to him in Hungarian, as the boy clung to her skirts.

Soon another guard came and herded all the immigrants inside a large building. There were rows of wooden benches, and the people were told to sit down and wait.

At the far end of the room, there was a long table, with desks flanking it on all sides. Back of the table there sat a number of United States Immigration officials dressed in uniform. They were filing cards and papers. They were doing their best to bring order out of this hodgepodge, to find out the names and histories of the newcomers, to determine who had relatives in this country, and to check passports and papers according to the laws of the United States. It was a formidable task, and it would take time.

About an hour later, one of the officials was talking to an old man. He had been trying, without success, to get some information from the oldster. The Russian interpreter was busy at another desk. The official could make no headway. Being a conscientious fellow, he wanted to get on, and so he turned to the roomful of people and called out, "Does anyone here speak Russian?"

A well-dressed, prim-looking young woman arose. "Sir," she said, in a shy but clear voice, "may I be of assistance?"

She had been sitting among a knot of finely dressed women at the side of the room. They were a group of socially minded New York matrons who had formed a welfare committee to visit Ward's Island.

"Why, I didn't know Emma knew Russian!" exclaimed one of the women, as she turned to another of the group. "I thought Emma was born here."

"Yes, indeed she was," answered her companion. "Right here in New York City, but she speaks Russian fluently."

The young lady walked toward the desk and introduced herself to the official.

"I am Emma Lazarus," she said quietly. "What do you wish me to do?"

The official explained that he wanted to get the old

man's story; where he was born, why he left Europe, and how he intended to make a living.

*"Strasvitche. Vasha imya?"* Emma asked. "Hello. What's your name?"

The old man beamed with delight at hearing his own language in this distant, strange land. He poured out his story.

His name was Abraham Rabinovitch. He came from the Crimea, a warm, rich area in southern Russia, where he had owned fertile farm lands. He had been born in the Crimea and had lived there for sixty-odd years. The peasants in that region had suffered great hardships and injustice. The Czar's government had been very oppressive. The peasants, somewhat hopelessly, somewhat desperately, had turned to the government with complaints, with demands—yes, at times, even with threats. The corrupt Russian officials had no intention of instituting any reforms. Instead, they determined to steer the discontent into other channels. The Russian officials told the peasants that the Jews were responsible for their misfortunes. They pointed out that some Jews had extensive farm land. The peasants were poor, illiterate, and, for the most part, woefully ignorant. They did not realize that there were a number of landowners of their own faith who were far richer than any Jews, and that there were a vast number of Jews who were just as poverty-stricken as most Crimean peasants. The Russian officials, trying

*"Sir," she said, in a shy but clear voice,*
*"may I be of assistance?"*

to hide the true cause of the poverty and misery, continually stirred up the peasants with false propaganda.

Finally, a riot broke out. Abraham's lands were confiscated by a mob. His two sons appealed to the chief of police. For their pains, they were arrested and charged with treason.

Abraham did not know their fate when he was forced to flee for his life. He escaped to Turkey, made his way to Italy, and finally managed to get to England, where he earned enough money to sail to America. He had a nephew somewhere in New York who, he was certain, would help him. Could the official locate this missing relative?

Emma Lazarus listened carefully to this heartbreaking tale, and then translated it for the immigration official.

"Tell him we will do our best," the official said, "and say we will keep him here in the meantime. You can't throw an old man like him out on the city in the dead of winter."

Emma relayed what the official said. Tears fell from the old man's eyes. He said it was the first free lodging he had been offered since he had been driven from his home.

Who was this woman who had come that day, at such a good time, to Ward's Island? Emma Lazarus was a writer and a poet who had been reared in a rather well-to-do family in New York. She had lived a very sheltered life, and had spent most of her time in the world of books.

But that day on Ward's Island had opened her eyes. The sheer shock of seeing such multitudes of unfortunates made her tremble. In the months to come, she was to spend many days at Ward's Island, and every day she would learn of new tragedies: people oppressed in Germany, in Italy, in Bosnia, in Poland; people fleeing from all corners of the wretched world; people running away from their native lands to this new shining heaven called America.

On they came, the old and the young, the old in gratefulness and the young in hope. And what energy they brought! Steel-muscled arms that dug mines and built subways; unceasing toil and inventive brains that started new industries; and above all, a gleaming pride in this, their newly adopted country, the land of freedom and democracy.

And so, when her old friend, Mr. William E. Evarts, came to her home one day at the head of a delegation to ask for her help in raising money for a pedestal for the Statue of Liberty, Emma Lazarus said she would be honored to be of any assistance.

What was this Statue of Liberty? People had been talking about it for years. Almost twenty years before, two Frenchmen had conceived the idea. They were Laboulaye, the statesman, and Bartholdi, the sculptor. They had dreamed of this idea, talked it over, and finally enlisted support throughout France. They had been ashamed, these two Frenchmen, of the unfriendly policies of the second French Empire toward America; and they thought it would be a fine gesture of friendship for France to send, as a gift, an enormous statue to the people of the United States, a statue symbolizing liberty. The French had toppled their king and the oppressive nobles from power with the slogan of *"Liberté! Egalité! Fraternité!"* Surely, the people of America who valued these words would welcome this statue. Did they not, too, practice the ideals of "Liberty! Equality! Fraternity!"? Did they not invite to their shores the oppressed of the world? Did not their Declaration of Independence say that all men are created equal?

But when the statue was accepted, it was found that no base had been provided on which to mount the huge figure. The French kept the statue in an immense shed in Paris. It would be sent over very soon, and provision had to be made for its erection in a suitable spot.

And what place could be more suitable than New York Harbor, the welcomer of immigrants? Bedloe's Island was chosen, and a committee appointed to raise funds for the pedestal. Manuscripts penned by such famous writers as Longfellow, Walt Whitman, Bret Harte, and Mark Twain were to be sold at auction. Since she was known in the literary world, Emma was asked by Mr. Evarts to contribute a manuscript.

What would Emma write about? What else but of the statue itself. She as much as anyone knew what this beacon light would mean to the unfortunates who fled Europe for the salvation of America.

She called her sonnet "The New Colossus."

History tells us that the Greeks built a statue so gigantic that it had one foot placed on one island and the other foot planted on another, with the sea running between the massive legs. It was known as the Colossus of Rhodes, and was accounted as one of the seven wonders of the ancient world. Emma Lazarus chose to call the Statue of Liberty the *new* Colossus. She said that the statue of "liberty enlightening the world," though not so big, was much more meaningful than the Greek statue. She told in stirring words what the Statue of Liberty meant to all peoples:

### THE NEW COLOSSUS

*Not like the brazen giant of Greek fame,*
*With conquering limbs astride from land to land;*
*Here at our sea-washed, sunset gates shall stand*
*A mighty woman with a torch, whose flame*
*Is the imprisoned lightning, and her name*
*Mother of Exiles. From her beacon-hand*
*Glows world-wide welcome; her mild eyes*
    *command*

*"Here at our sea-washed, sunset gates shall stand*
*A mighty woman with a torch . . ."*

*The air-bridged harbor that twin cities frame.*
*"Keep, ancient lands, your storied pomp!" cries*
    *she*
*With silent lips. "Give me your tired, your poor,*
*Your huddled masses yearning to breathe free,*
*The wretched refuse of your teeming shore.*
*Send these, the homeless, tempest-tost to me!*
*I lift my lamp beside the golden door."*

This famous poem has become a part of world literature. In 1903, in loving memory of the noted poetess who wrote these inspiring words, a group of admiring citizens requested that this sonnet be engraved upon the pedestal of the Statue of Liberty. There you will find these words today—as meaningful as they ever were to the people who sing:

> *"My country 'tis of thee,*
> *Sweet land of liberty . . .*
> *Let freedom ring!"*

# JULIETTE LOW
## Founder of the Girl Scouts

IT WAS A glittering dinner party, the kind that the English do so well. Titled gentlemen and ladies were present, jewels sparkled, and the entire atmosphere was elegance itself. But if you had looked closely, you would have noticed a charming-looking, middle-aged woman who was not really enjoying herself.

Some might have thought it was because Juliette Low was an American—a native of Savannah, Georgia—and that she did not feel at home in English society. But this was not the real reason. Juliette's husband had been an Englishman. They had lived for years on a beautiful English country estate where they entertained lavishly, and most of the people at this dinner party were old friends of hers. Others, who noticed that the lady was somewhat deaf in both ears, might have attributed her apparent loneliness to this affliction. But her close friends could have told them that Juliette had long ago learned to live with her disability, and that, on the contrary, she had always been one of the gayest and most vivacious of women.

No, the truth was that Juliette felt deeply the loss of her husband. After their exciting life of travels around the world, of constant social gatherings—without her life companion—she felt so terribly alone in the world. A woman who adored children, she had none of her own. Neither her love for animals nor her interest in art seemed capable anymore of filling up her life. There no longer seemed to be purpose in her life.

But Juliette Low was destined to find her purpose at this very party—a purpose to which she would dedicate the rest of her life. And it all began because her hostess introduced her to the famous Sir Robert Baden-Powell, founder of the Boy Scout movement.

"Sir Robert, I do envy you so," said Juliette. "You have made such a great success of everything. Your achievement with the Boy Scouts has been marvelous, and it will live on for centuries, bringing knowledge and pleasure and goodness into people's lives. I feel that my life is being wasted, and I don't know what to do about it."

"Though we are sometimes unaware," Sir Robert said, "Providence always guides us to the right path.

*. . . jewels sparkled, and the entire atmosphere*
*was elegance itself.*

You will know what direction to take when your opportunity arises."

And then he went on to tell her about his organization—of how Scouting promoted friendship, built character, trained the boys in citizenship and in various skills.

Juliette's imagination caught fire as she listened to this dedicated man. How wonderful it must be for boys all over the world to participate in Scouting! *But why should girls be left out?* And she finally voiced the question that had been perplexing her. "Is there any reason, Sir Robert, why there could not be a similar organization for girls? They need to learn all these same things; they need guidance and fellowship. Why can't we provide these for them?"

"But, my dear lady," Sir Robert replied, "we have already started such an organization. At our Boy Scout rally in 1909, we were suddenly confronted with a whole troop of the boys' sisters, who demanded 'equal rights,' so to speak. And now, in order to meet their needs, we have launched a program called the English Girl Guides."

That was all she needed to hear. During the next year, Mrs. Low learned everything she could about the Girl Guide movement. Then she organized her own troop in Scotland. Since most of the girls came from poor homes, she decided to teach them practical skills like gardening, cooking, weaving—things that would help them in rearing their own families someday. She also arranged for plenty of parties and fun. She was thrilled to see how much good these activities seemed to be doing for the girls. What's more, she herself realized that she was once again happy, that by giving herself to others, she could forget her sorrow and satisfy her longing for accomplishment.

After organizing a troop in London and talking with various leaders throughout England, she felt ready to bring this inspiring new movement back across the ocean to America. When she arrived in Savannah, she could hardly wait to tell her family and friends about her plans.

Imagine her disappointment at their lukewarm reaction. Her mother said, "Juliette, dear, remember that you're fifty-two years old now. This kind of work will be too great a strain on you." And a nephew said, "You have no training at all in organizational work or in business. And you know what a poor head you have for figures. How would you ever manage the finances?"

What no one said—though Juliette knew it was uppermost in their minds—was: Don't forget that you're partially deaf. How can you expect to work with a bunch of young girls?

Juliette Low was undaunted. She invited eight local girls to come to her house for tea. When she had told them about the English Girl Guides, the response was tremendously enthusiastic. "Well, girls, how would you

like to form a troop of our own right here in Savannah?"
she asked.

She was greeted with cries of "Yes, yes!" and questions like "Will you teach us how to swim?" and "Can
we go on hikes?" For a while, it was a real bedlam, such
was the excitement of the girls. They screamed and
laughed and chattered and danced about for sheer
pleasure.

But Juliette interrupted the celebration.

"First of all, I can see that we must learn discipline.
Calm down, girls, and we'll talk about our activities.
We'll meet here in the carriage house, and the vacant
lot next door can be used for games. We'll have fun, and
we'll also do things to help other people. We'll all sew
our own uniforms. Now all of you raise your right
hands and repeat after me: We promise to serve God
and country, to be courteous, obedient, trustworthy,
loyal, and helpful."

And so the organization of the Girl Scouts of America was born. Despite the enthusiasm of the girls, at first
there was considerable opposition from their parents.
This kind of thing was all right for rough-and-ready
boys, but it somehow didn't seem right for respectable
girls to go on camping trips, to learn how to tie knots, or
to participate actively in sports. Nice little girls should
only do those things that were perfectly ladylike.

But the parents gradually realized what Mrs. Low was
accomplishing. They saw their daughters learn impor-

tant things while they were having fun. And they respected the guiding principle of the Girl Scout leader: that a Girl Scout is a friend to all and helps other people at all times.

Juliette Low conducted a one-woman crusade in those first struggling days of Scouting. She enlisted the aid of prominent people and friends all over the country. She traveled from community to community, giving lectures on the value of her organization: how it better prepared girls for active, purposeful lives, and how it helped the lonely and the insecure. Her charming manner made it possible for her to enlist all kinds of support.

By 1913, troops had been formed throughout the country, a *Girl Scout Handbook* had been published, and a national headquarters opened in Washington. When the United States entered World War I, the Girl Scouts had the chance to prove their ability to serve community and country. They knitted sweaters for overseas troops, raised vegetable gardens, canned, worked at recreation centers, served as Red Cross messengers, and helped with Liberty Loan drives. Scouting really came into its own at this time, and the membership rolls grew by leaps and bounds. Mrs. Woodrow Wilson, wife of the President, appeared wearing a Girl Scout uniform; Mrs. Low and several Girl Scouts were received at the White House; and the nation paid tribute to its gallant young girls.

The movement continued to grow after the war.

*Each girl placed a bundle of twigs on the campfire . . . .*

Then, in 1926, another of Juliette's dreams came true when the World Camp of Girl Guides was held in America for the first time. Delegates from thirty-one nations assembled for the exciting occasion—East Indian girls in saris, Czech girls in embroidered skirts and blouses, Japanese girls in kimonos. Each girl placed a bundle of twigs upon the huge campfire to symbolize her nation's gift to the world. Sir Robert Baden-Powell spoke to the assembly, urging them, "Go from here full of the thought that you are going to promote peace and good will." And Juliette Low was proud and happy that she had been able to live long enough to view this inspiring spectacle.

She died the following year, content in the knowledge that she had achieved her purpose in life. This wonderful lady who dedicated her life to young girls has received many tributes—ships and schools have been named after her, a three-cent stamp was issued in her honor, her birthplace and childhood home has been restored as a national Girl Scout center. But her memory is best preserved in the lives of the more than two million American Girl Scouts who are dedicated to the high ideals she set down for them.

# JANE ADDAMS
## Crusader Against Poverty

MRS. MORAN stood huddled against the side of a building on a street corner in Chicago. The rain was coming down in torrents, and the poor woman was already soaked through to the skin. But it was not herself she was concerned about; it was the paper bags containing beans and flour, which she clutched against her body in a desperate effort to keep them dry. For only these pitiful bits of food stood between her children and starvation! She had walked many long blocks to get her weekly share of rations from the County Agent's office, and now she was afraid the food would all be spoiled.

When a streetcar stopped at the corner, she impulsively dashed aboard it, knowing she had no money to pay the fare, but hoping that somehow she might be able to go at least part of the way home. The scene that followed probably looked highly comical to some spectators, but it was tragic for Mrs. Moran. Her sopping-wet paper bags suddenly burst; beans rolled all over the floor of the streetcar, and clouds of white flour floated through the air, settling mischievously on the ladies' dresses.

"Horrible woman!" one of the ladies shrieked. "Come here this instant, and dust my clothes off. You've ruined them." And then the other fine ladies began screaming at her. The conductor, too, joined the chorus. "Why can't you watch what you're doing, lady? This ain't no grocery store! I could have you arrested for disturbing the passengers. And by the way, where's your fare?"

"I'm sorry, mister," Mrs. Moran said weakly, "but I don't have any money."

"Is that so? Well, now, ain't that a cryin' shame!" the conductor replied. "We'll just stop right here, and be off with you, madame. And thank your stars that I'm not turnin' you in. The Chicago streetcars ain't runnin' no public charity, you know."

Mrs. Moran was seething with rage as she stepped off the streetcar, and her heart sank as she realized that her precious food was gone. Then she noticed that she had been let off right in front of a big old mansion that was surrounded on all sides by crowded, dreary tenement houses. She had heard a great deal from her friends about Miss Addams, the mistress of Hull House, who welcomed all her poverty-stricken neighbors into her grand mansion and dispensed not only hospitality and kindness but help. Since the rain had not yet let up, Mrs. Moran thought she might as well take this opportunity to visit Miss Addams.

She was warmly welcomed by a lady whose face and manner radiated kindness. "Oh, my dear, come with me to the fire," Jane Addams said. "We'll get you dried off, and give you a nice cup of hot tea that will make you feel much better. And please don't worry about your food. We'll scrape together some provisions for your children."

As they sat together sipping tea and talking, Mrs. Moran felt no shame in telling her problems to this sympathetic lady. She poured out her anger against the "cursed poverty" that blighted so many thousands of people in the city, and against the politicians who gave out a thimbleful of charity here and there, but did nothing to really improve conditions.

Jane Addams understood this story well, because she had been fighting poverty, disease, hunger, and ignorance all her life. It had all begun when, as a seven-year-old girl, she had gone with her father, a wealthy mill-owner, to visit the miserable slums where the mill-workers lived.

Terribly upset by what she saw, Jane asked her father, "Papa, why do the people live in such horrid places?"

Her father tried to explain the facts of poverty, telling her that some fortunate people like themselves had enough money to live comfortably and to buy all the luxuries they wanted, while others—less fortunate, but still good people—were too poor to afford anything more than the most basic necessities to keep their bodies alive.

Little Jane's eyes blazed as she thought of this terrible injustice, and she made a solemn vow. "When I grow up, Papa, I want to live in a nice house just like ours, but I want it to be on a street like this, between horrid little houses like these. And I'll invite all the poor people into my great house and give them whatever I can."

Jane Addams was true to her word. When she was ready to enter college, she decided to be a doctor, believing that she could contribute most if she had the medical knowledge and skill to relieve the suffering and disease of the poor. But her own delicate health forced her to give up the grueling routine of medical school. During a trip to Europe, where her doctors had ordered her to go for rest and recuperation, she observed the slums and poverty of the Old World, and found them neither better nor worse than those of Chicago.

She returned home knowing that the time had come for her to begin her war against poverty. She and a friend, Ellen Starr, rented Hull House in 1889 and con-

*"Papa, why do the people live in such horrid places?"*

verted it into a community service center for the thousands of underprivileged immigrants who lived in the
area. There were Italians, Germans, Russian and Polish
Jews, Irish—all crowded into their separate settlements
of rotten tenements, filthy stables and outhouses,
saloons, and dives. The neighborhoods seethed with
crime and corruption. Each group hated the others, having brought their prejudices with them from the old
countries. Here was a tough assignment for two well-

bred young ladies.

At first, the people distrusted this rich lady who offered them friendship and help. Why should she want to come and live among them? What did she expect to get out of them?

But they soon realized that she only wanted to help. Her many deeds of kindness, her indomitable courage, her unceasing work earned her the complete respect of all who met or heard about her. Jane Addams fought corrupt politicians in behalf of clean streets; she fought crime and evil in all forms; she took an interest in labor problems and supported a movement to abolish sweat shops; she helped to establish a Juvenile Court; and she was instrumental in the opening of playgrounds and vacation schools. She even served the city for three years as a district inspector of streets and alleys.

The fame of Jane Addams' work spread throughout the world. Social workers followed her shining example to bring relief to the slums of many other cities. Thousands of miserable men, women, and children were made healthier, happier, and better because of her.

Hull House grew from the one old house to a community center of thirteen buildings. Among the services offered there were a kindergarten for children, a gymnasium, handicrafts, music, various clubs and classes. The center still operates today on Chicago's West Side, staffed by friends and associates who follow in the path of Jane Addams.

Though Jane Addams devoted forty years of her life to her labor of love at Hull House, she also managed to find time for active participation in other causes. She was at the forefront of the women's movements to bring about peace, and was elected first President of the Women's International League for Peace in 1915. She had made warring nationalities in Chicago forget their old grudges, and she hoped to do the same among the nations of Europe. She traveled from one country to another, striving to convince the world leaders to end the war through negotiation. Though unsuccessful, her efforts did rally worldwide attention to the cause of peace. And after the war, she directed her energies toward helping the defenseless victims of war: the women and children.

In 1931, Jane Addams was awarded the Nobel Peace Prize, the highest recognition that can be bestowed on a great humanitarian. It must have given her new hope that the world she had worked so hard to bring about—a world of equal opportunity, a world of peace—might yet come. In bestowing the award, the Chairman of the Committee addressed her as *America's Uncrowned Queen.*

And so she was—one of the great, noble American women of all time. Her memory lives on in cities throughout the world—in the community houses that attempt to help underprivileged people find a richer and more satisfying life.

# LILLIAN WALD
## *Pioneer Social Worker*

THE CLASSROOM was so small and so crowded that two women shared every seat. And those who could find no place to sit, stood against the wall. The cries of the pushcart peddlers and children rose from the street below and filled the room. The teacher almost had to shout to be heard.

The teacher, a pretty, brown-eyed young woman, was bending over a bed that stood in the front of the classroom. "Now, my friends," she said, "you have all been making beds for years. But there are ways and ways of making a bed. First of all, the sheets must be tucked in tightly—like this—if the bed is to be comfortable and neat. Then, the mattress must be turned over at least once a week if it is to keep its shape. And,

of course, you know that you should give all the bedclothes a good airing regularly."

A woman spoke up from the rear of the room. "Say,
Miss Wald, it's easy to see you ain't been in this neighborhood long. How we going to air the beds if there
ain't no windows in the bedrooms?"

The women pupils burst out laughing, and Miss
Wald, the teacher, joined them.

When the laugher died down, the teacher, still
smiling, said, "You're right, Mrs. Bronsky. I know it's
hard to get enough fresh air here even to *breathe,* but
you should move the bedclothes into a room that has
a window. Or even better—carry them up to the roof
on a sunny day. You see—"

At that point, the door of the classroom opened
slowly. Everyone turned to look at the latecomer. But
instead of another adult student, there stood an eight-
year-old girl. Her face was dirty and streaked with
tears.

Miss Wald went over to her quickly. "Why, my
dear, come in. What is the matter?"

The little girl appeared frightened and embarrassed.
Every eye was on her, and she could hardly speak.

"Don't be frightened, my child," Miss Wald said,
bending down before the child and taking one of the
girl's hands in hers. "Tell me why you are crying. Can
I help you?"

The little girl looked down at her shoes and sobbed

as she spoke. "It's my mother, Miss Wald. She sent me to see if you'd come. She's sick in bed."

"Of course I will, my dear." Miss Wald stood up and turned to the class. "That will be all for today, ladies. I'll see you all here again next week. Good morning."

A few moments later, Miss Wald was in the street with the little girl. She carried a small black case in her hand, and under her arm was a package of fresh bed linen. Lillian Wald was a trained nurse, as well as a teacher, and once a week she conducted a free class in home nursing. The lessons were given in a tiny house on Henry Street in New York City.

Lillian held the child's hand as they stepped over the garbage-filled gutters. The streets and sidewalks were crowded with pushcarts, shawl-wrapped women, and heavily bearded men. The air was heavy with the smell of squalor.

Hand in hand, the teacher and the little girl hurried along the narrow, winding streets. "Tell me what the trouble is," Lillian said gently.

"My mother's so sick, Miss Wald, that she can't get up. All my brothers and sisters are crying. We didn't know what to do."

"How many brothers and sisters do you have, my child?"

"Five, Miss Wald. I'm the oldest."

"And where's your father, child?"

"He's dead, ma'am."

Lillian patted the little girl's head. "Never mind, my dear. We'll take care of everything. You don't have to worry now."

At that moment, an old fish peddler called out, "Hey, Miss Wald." He waved to them from under the huge umbrella that rose from his pushcart.

Lillian and the child stopped. "Hello, Abraham. How are you today?"

"I'm fine, Miss Wald, just fine. Please, Miss Wald, would you do me a favor?"

"Of course, Abraham, if I can," Lillian said, smiling.

"Let me give you some fish. Business has been very good and I'd like to give you some fish. I have some fine, fresh carp here," the peddler said eagerly.

"That's awfully nice of you, Abraham, but you must let me pay for them."

"*You,* Miss Wald? Pay for them? Not for *my* fish, Miss Wald," said the old man in mock outrage. "You could never pay us for anything with money." He began to wrap up two large fish. "Last night, when the other peddlers and I came to see you at your house, you treated us like important people. We'll remember that, Miss Wald." The old man's eyes filled with tears as he handed Lillian the package.

"Well, thank you, Abraham. This is very kind of you. I have to hurry off now. But I'll see you and your friends again, soon, about that matter." Lillian waved to the peddler and went quickly on her way.

The night before, a delegation of fish peddlers had come to her home to ask for help in protecting their rights as small businessmen. At the time, she was entertaining guests for dinner. Lillian wanted the peddlers to come in and join her, but they refused. They felt they couldn't talk in front of strangers.

"But you, Miss Wald," explained the spokesman, "we can talk to *you*. You're as good as a fish peddler. At least you can feel like a fish peddler."

Lillian considered that one of the finest compliments she had ever received.

Finally, Lillian arrived at the child's home. Flight after flight, they climbed up the dark, creaking stairs.

*"You, Miss Wald? Pay for them? Not for my fish,"*
*said the old man in mock outrage.*

The smells that filled the tenement halls made Lillian hold her breath. At the head of the fourth flight, the little girl opened a door. Lillian followed her in.

The apartment had just two rooms. In a corner, on a dirty, unmade cot, lay the sick woman. It was Mrs. Gordon, one of Lillian's adult students. Without a word, Lillian opened her black bag. She put a thermometer in the woman's mouth and took her pulse. When she had finished, the woman whispered weakly, "Thank you for coming, Miss Wald. I don't know what we would have done."

Lillian put her hand on the woman's forehead. "That's all right, my dear. I'm glad you sent for me."

Mrs. Gordon's temperature was not high. From her thin arms and tired face, Lillian knew that she was underfed and badly overworked. How could anyone be living this way!

Lillian helped Mrs. Gordon to a chair, then made the bed with the clean linen she had brought. In a few minutes, Mrs. Gordon was back in bed, tucked in and peaceful.

"Now, you close your eyes and rest. I'll take care of everything," Lillian said. Almost immediately, the woman passed into a much-needed sleep.

Lillian looked around the room. The only light came from a single gas jet. There was no heat; there was no hot water. Only one of the two rooms had a small window, and that opened out on a brick wall less than two feet away. Little chance was there for sunshine or a breeze of fresh air to enter.

Lillian noticed some rough wooden planks against the wall. Turning to the child who had brought her, she asked what they were for.

"Oh, that's where we sleep, Miss Wald," the child said. "We only have one bed."

Lillian said nothing, so that the child would not know how sick the sight of this kind of life made her feel. And this was typical of the tenements in the lower East Side of New York City in the year 1893. Besides being dark and dreary, many of these tenement flats were almost unbearably hot in summer because they were crowded so closely together. In winter, they were very cold, for most tenants could not afford coal or wood to heat them, and a fire burned only when a meal was being prepared. Quite often, there was no fuel even to cook a hot meal or to heat water.

Few of the individual flats had running water. People were lucky if there was one cold-water tap on each floor. Tenants usually had to go all the way to the ground floor for every drop of water they used. Bathrooms were almost unheard of. Sometimes there was a single inside toilet that had to be shared by an entire houseful of families, but more often there was only an outside privy in a tiny, dirty yard.

Instead of being discouraged, Lillian rolled up her sleeves. She heated tubs of water on the stove. After

*Lillian noticed some wooden planks . . . she asked what they were for.*

she had bathed each child and dressed them as best she could in their ragged clothes, she attacked the floors, the walls, the furniture. She scrubbed and cleaned all day long. And when she had finished, the place had taken on a new look.

Giving the oldest child money, she sent her to the store for vegetables and fruit. And with the fish that Abraham had given her, Lillian prepared the first good meal the family had had in months.

After one of the hardest days of her life, Lillian left the Gordons, promising to return the next day. Thus began the Public Health Nursing Service. For Lillian, shocked by the desperate need of these poor unfortunates, organized a group of trained nurses who would go into peoples' homes and nurse them, regardless of whether they could pay for the care or not.

Lillian did not stop there. She opened the first *settlement house* in New York, on Henry Street. This was a place where people could come to talk over their problems, or learn such things as carpentry and nursing and child care. There were a kindergarten, gymnasium, dancing school, debating club, and literary society. The house on Henry Street became the center of the neighborhood.

Beginning with this little organization, many new social ideas grew and developed in New York. Public nursing became an accepted institution throughout the city. School lunches, the Neighborhood Playhouse on

Grand Street, laws to protect children—all these stemmed from the Henry Street Settlement House.

At the center of this activity was Lillian Wald. She came to be known, loved, and respected by all the poor people of the lower East Side. The toughest fellows in the neighborhood protected her at all hours, so it was never dangerous for her to make her rounds, even when she was called out in the middle of the night. A Chinese friend of Lillian's once called her "Heavenly Lady Number One."

When the city opened a new playground on Cherry Street in 1937, it was dedicated to Lillian Wald "in appreciation of her pioneer work for children and district nursing in this city." Lillian was pleased. She knew the playground would mean so much to the East Side and to her old neighbors.

She would have been even more pleased had she lived to see the fine groups of buildings that the city of New York erected in her memory just a few years ago. It is a housing development along the East River in the very heart of the lower East Side. Lillian would have been overjoyed to see the cleanliness and charm of the apartments, in which every room has light and air. The project is called the Lillian Wald Houses.

People will always love and remember Lillian Wald because she did so much for others. Only from a truly great and noble heart could come such a desire to help the unfortunate.

# AMELIA EARHART
## *America's Great Aviatrix*

ONE DAY, four children were playing in a backyard in the small town of Atchison, Kansas. Theirs was a strange and fascinating game. Instead of playing house or sewing doll clothes, like other nice little girls, these four were building a roller coaster! Their materials were very simple: old clapboards, fence rails, wheels of discarded roller skates. When the homemade roller coaster was completed, the youngest girl asked excitedly:

"Now, where shall we start?"

"The roof, of course," an older girl answered decisively. "From the ridgepole." She was slender and golden-haired, a little taller than the others, obviously the leader of the group.

"I'll be the first to try," she calmly offered.

"Be careful, Amelia!" the others chorused. "You'll get hurt."

But with a laugh and a toss of her blond hair, Amelia climbed aboard. On the first try, the roller coaster overturned. Car and driver landed in a heap on the ground. The other children gasped. But Amelia got to her feet, unhurt, laughing harder than ever.

"I'm going to try again!" she declared.

This time Amelia took off like a bird and made a perfect three-point landing.

"Did you see?" Amelia cried joyfully. "It's—why, it's like flying! *I flew!*"

That was Amelia Earhart's first flight.

From the very beginning, Amelia was different from other girls. The caption under her picture in the high school yearbook read, "The girl in brown, who walks alone." Indeed she did.

She was enchanted by airplanes and flying. She spent every free moment away from school at nearby airfields, watching in fascination as planes landed and took off. Once, she even took a course in engine repairing!

She attended an air meet at Long Beach. Her sharp eyes spotted a pilot.

"Father," she whispered, "please go over and ask that man how much it costs to learn to fly."

It cost a thousand dollars!

Right then and there, Amelia Earhart determined to

*. . . Amelia took off like a bird.*

learn how to fly—no matter what the price! She would earn the money.

Her aptitude at the controls amazed even the experts. After only ten hours of instruction, she made her first solo flight! Shortly afterwards, she set an altitude record of 14,000 feet.

Later, she received an invitation to fly the Atlantic. It was in 1928, while she was doing social work in Boston, that she received the phone call that changed her whole life. The man on the other end of the line was Wilbur Stultz. Wilbur was a pilot who planned to fly across the ocean in a plane called *The Friendship*. Amelia jumped at Stultz's invitation to join the crew as its only woman member.

*The Friendship* took off from Trepassey Bay, Newfoundland on June 17, 1928. Just twenty hours and forty minutes later, the aircraft landed in Great Britain!

From that day on, Amelia Earhart was a celebrity. Flying, which had always been in her blood, now became her life. She determined to be the first woman to fly the Atlantic alone!

On May 20, 1932, Amelia Earhart took off from Harbor Grace in Newfoundland with only the clothes on her back, a thermos of coffee, a can of tomato juice, a comb, and a toothbrush.

In the record time of thirteen hours and thirty minutes, she landed in a pasture in Londonderry, Ireland. To the astonished farmer who ran up to welcome this solitary birdwoman in windbreaker and jodhpurs, Amelia Earhart's greeting was characteristically simple:

"Hello," she said. "I've come from America."

For this achievement, Amelia Earhart was decorated by the French and American governments. She was awarded the Distinguished Flying Cross and the special Gold Medal of the National Geographic Society. From then on, her thirst to conquer the skies and establish new aviation records became even more intense.

In January, 1935, she flew from Hawaii to Oakland, California—the first woman to make the flight. In May of the same year, she flew nonstop from Mexico City to New York City. The time: fourteen hours, nineteen minutes.

Amelia could not remain earthbound for long. She longed to prove again and again that the unspoiled highways of the heavens belonged to *women* flyers, as well as men.

"I have a feeling," she told a friend, "that there is just one more good flight left in my system. Anyway, when I have finished this job, I mean to give up major long-distance flights."

The "one more good flight" was to be an around-the-world attempt over the equator.

Like the first flight in the roller coaster years before, Amelia's first try at an around-the-world record was unsuccessful. She flew from California to Hawaii, but cracked up as she was taking off from Honolulu on the

*"Hello," she said, "I've come from America."*

second lap of her trip. So she returned to the U.S., determined to try again.

On June 1, 1937, she took off with Fred Noonan as navigator, from Miami, Florida. Several weeks later, they landed in Lae, New Guinea. From Lae, the two set their course for Howland, a tiny island in the Pacific.

On July 3, the day following the take-off from Lae, a message was picked up by the Coast Guard cutter *Ithaca*. Amelia and Fred were in trouble.

Amelia Earhart had been right. This was indeed her last flight. Though U.S. Navy vessels searched for a week in the waters off Howland Island, no trace was found of even the wreckage.

The whole world mourned the loss of America's gallant aviatrix. But a bird cannot be happy anywhere but in the air, and everyone knew that Amelia Earhart went exactly as she would have wished to go. This woman with wings sought to conquer the skies. That was her life and her achievement.

Five years earlier, President Herbert Hoover had presented her with the Gold Medal of the National Geographic Society. He had commended her for her generous work in "expanding the paths of women." As modest as she was brave, Amelia Earhart had replied, "I shall be happy if my small exploit has drawn attention to the fact that women, too, are flying."

Who can doubt that it did!

# HELEN KELLER
## Conqueror of Darkness

COULD YOU IMAGINE living in a world that was pitch-dark and absolutely silent? You would not know what your father or mother looked like, or even how you looked yourself! You would never have heard a dog bark, or any other sound. You would not know how to talk, because you would have never heard a word spoken. In fact, you would not know that there were such things as *words!*

You would have no idea of sunshine, except to feel its warmth. You would have no idea of right and wrong, because no one would have ever been able to explain that to you. You would not understand that something was yours, or that it belonged to someone else, because no one would have any means of communicating with you except to *touch* you.

This was the kind of world in which Helen Keller lived.

When Helen was born, she was a normal, beautiful baby who could see and hear. But, at nineteen months of age, she became very ill, and her sickness left her blind and entirely deaf.

She had just begun to talk before the illness struck, but soon, in the darkness that enclosed her, she forgot the few words she had known. Except for a dim memory of sky and trees, she might as well have never seen anything.

"My poor baby," sobbed Mrs. Keller, "it's as if she were lost to us."

"We must spend our lives trying to make her happy," Mr. Keller replied, as he attempted to comfort his wife.

"But what can we do?" Mrs. Keller argued. "She can't see us. She can't speak to us. She can't hear us. We're helpless—helpless!"

As time passed, Helen did learn a few things. By the time she was five, she could recognize her own clothes and would put them away in her own bureau drawers. She had made up a sort of sign language, and her family could tell when she meant *Come, Go, Yes,* and *No.* When she touched her own cheek, it meant that she was referring to her mother. If she wanted something small, but a large object was given her, she would make her sign for "No." Then she would take a tiny bit of the skin·of one hand by the thumb and a finger of the other. Spreading her fingers wide and bringing her hands together meant she wanted the object—a piece of cake or whatever else—to be large.

And she was becoming a very naughty girl. Since no one could teach her anything, she became spoiled. Her father and mother, in efforts to make her happy, tried to think of everything she could want, and whenever she could make herself understood, her demands were instantly fulfilled.

You know how it is on a gloomy, rainy day, when you've read and played games until you're tired and bored and have nothing to do.

"What shall I do, Mother?" you say. "Think of something for me to do."

Now suppose you were enclosed in complete darkness and silence and you couldn't think of anything to do, but you couldn't even *ask* your mother to help you. You would be shut in, and there would be no way to get out.

Helen was indeed shut in. She had no possible way to get out, so she began to have temper tantrums. The few signs she had used became more and more inadequate, and every time she failed in expressing her wants, she became angry. Her father and mother knew that something must be done, for Helen was terribly unhappy and was making their life wretched as well.

Specialists had decided long ago that Helen's sight could never be restored. Finally, Helen's father was advised to write to Boston to the Perkins Institute for the Blind.

And one day, when Helen was not quite seven years old, a teacher came to help her. Her name was Anne Sullivan. She was not much more than a girl herself. She, too, had been almost totally blind, although now she could see quite well.

She set to work to try to release Helen from the darkness and silence in which she lived.

Anne began by spelling the word *doll* into Helen's hand when she gave her doll to the little girl. In this kind of talking, the speaker uses the single-hand alphabet generally used by the deaf. The blind listener lightly places her hand over that of the speaker and feels the words as they are spelled.

Helen didn't know what the finger movements meant, but it was something new, and she quickly imitated it. Soon, she realized that if she made those particular motions, the doll was put in her arms. But she didn't know that the movements meant the name *doll.* In fact, she didn't know that things even *had* names!

Helen was a very bright little girl, and she quickly learned to make a good many words. But still she didn't know that they meant anything except a way to get something she wanted.

And she continued to be very naughty, for she had never been taught to obey.

Anne decided that the very next thing she must teach Helen was obedience.

But how do you teach someone to mind when you can't talk to her or show her anything? There was only one way, and that was force. When Helen kicked and screamed and bit, Anne held her until she stopped. Helen was a healthy, strong girl, and sometimes these tussles lasted an hour or two. Anne would be exhausted, but she would not give up.

Gradually, Helen learned discipline. At the same time, she was learning more and more combinations of finger movements. But she still didn't know that they meant the names of things.

She had learned the combinations for *mug* and for *water,* but she kept getting them mixed up. One day, Anne took her into the garden and had Helen hold her hand under the spout of the pump in the well house. As the cold water gushed out over Helen's right hand, Anne spelled *water* into Helen's other hand.

Helen stood stock-still, while an expression of delight came over her face. At last she had understood. She spelled *water* several times. Then she dropped to the ground and made it plain that she wanted to know the name of that. Anne spelled it for her.

Helen had found the way out, and, once given the key to understanding, nothing could stop her. In a few hours, she learned thirty new words! She knew, at last, that they were the names of things.

From that day on, she progressed rapidly. Just as a baby learns to speak, Helen learned to make words. Then she began to make sentences. Soon the sentences became longer and more complicated.

Now, she could actually talk with anyone who understood finger spelling. Helen's father and mother learned it, so that they could talk with her.

The next step was to teach her to read. She already liked stories, for Anne would read to her by the hour, translating into finger spelling the words that she read from books.

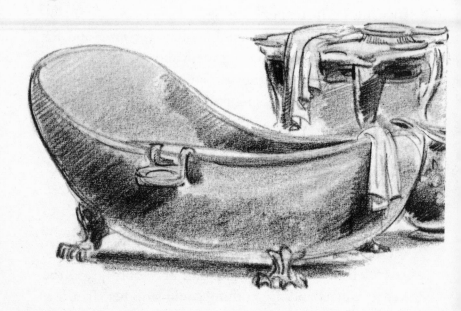

*When Helen kicked and screamed and bit,*
*Anne held her until she stopped.*

Helen was given books with raised letters, called *Braille,* and she soon learned to read them by passing her fingers over the letters. Helen's hands were to her what eyes and ears are to everyone else.

Of course, she could not speak, because she could not remember ever having heard speech. But the impulse to utter sounds was strong. She liked to feel the cat purr and the dog bark. She could "listen" to her pet rooster crow when he perched on her knee and she put her hand on his throat. She liked to put her hand on a singer's throat or on the piano when it was being played.

She liked to feel her mother's lips move, and she moved her own; although she couldn't talk, she made sounds. There was just one word that she remembered from the time before she was ill, and that was *wa-wa.* This, to her, meant she wanted a drink of water.

One day, a visitor told Helen by finger movements about a deaf girl who had learned to talk, and at once Helen was wild to learn. She was taken to the Horace Mann School for the Deaf in Boston, and there she got her first lessons in positioning her tongue and lips to make the sounds of speech.

Now another door was unlocked.

But there were still new fields to conquer. Helen wanted to go to school. This was felt to be quite impossible, but Helen persisted.

Anne went to all her classes with her; and patiently,

as the teacher spoke, Anne spelled everything into Helen's hand. Helen learned to use the typewriter so that she could prepare her lessons, and she learned to write and to read Braille—the system of raised dots in which most books for the blind are printed. She learned to swim, and to row, and to ride a bicycle.

In 1904, she was graduated from college with honors. Her life entered a new phase. She was no longer the child, loved by the whole country; she was now a woman, ready to rely upon her own abilities. Helen had wanted to be more than an unusual example of what a handicapped person could accomplish. To most people, she had always been a pitiful girl they read about in newspapers and magazines.

Helen now became a living legend. She was a great American success story. After her book, *The Story of My Life,* was published, she began a career of writing on behalf of those still shut off from a normal life. Her articles reached a wide audience. They brought her tremendous support.

Later, Helen realized that she could help the blind and deaf most by meeting the public, face to face. She had to mingle with people. She had to become a real flesh-and-blood person to win her fight for the handicapped.

Helen's greatest ordeal was her first appearance before an audience. She was very shy and quite terrified. But her determination and will carried her through.

*Helen's greatest ordeal was her first appearance
before an audience.*

With Anne, she went on lecture tours all over the
United States and Europe. Everywhere she went, she
enlisted aid for the blind and deaf. Today, she still
carries on this never-ending battle.

Helen Keller's unsurpassed courage enabled her to
conquer a world of darkness. She has lived to take a
most honored place in the world she once feared.

HART

PUBLISHING

COMPANY